MUSIC:
THE WAY I SEE IT

A COMPREHENSIVE STUDY
IN THE MAJOR SCALE

WRITTEN, ILLUSTRATED, & EDITED
BY JAY McGEE

PUBLISHED BY MORE POWER PUBLISHING

TABLE OF CONTENTS

Foreword

If you have purchased this book, congratulations on taking an important step toward your quest to become musically empowered. By following the instructions, as directed, you will most definitely learn to understand music. Whether you're seeking a career in music, just wish to entertain yourself or small gatherings, or want to teach others, you are on the right course. You will find this book unlike any other in it's simplicity and depth. By that, we mean that we will try to explain everything completely; and leave you wondering about nothing that we touch on, lesson-wise.

Sincerely,

Jay McGee

Email: jaymcgee23@gmail.com

Chapter 1

<u>Major Scales</u>

   Western music, meaning music of the western world, music based upon the diatonic, otherwise called, the major scale: (pop, c&w, blues, gospel, jazz, r&b, classical, etc.) uses seven letters from the English language.

   Those letters (notes) are A B C D E F G (white keys). The only variables (other forms) are:

    (A♯ B♭)(C♯ D♭)(D♯ E♭)(F♯ G♭)(G♯ A♭)
    (found on the black keys).

 (1) (2) (3) (4)(5)(6) (7) (8) (9)(10)(11) (12)(13) (14)(15)

A B C D E F G A B C D E F G A B C D E F G A

<u>Notes found on the black keys:</u>

(1) A♯/B♭ (2) C♯/D♭ (3) D♯/E♭ (4) F♯/G♭ (5) G♯/A♭

(6) A♯/B♭ (7) C♯/D♭ (8) D♯/E♭ (9) F♯/G♭ (10) G♯/A♭

(11) A♯/B♭ (12) C♯/D♭ (13) D♯/E♭ (14) F♯/G♭ (15) G♯/A♭

* If a black key comes after (to the right of) a white key, it is called the sharp of the white key; if a black key comes before (to the left of) a white key, it is called the flat of the white key.

Here is one way to familiarize yourself with the names of the notes on a keyboard.

The two white keys with no black keys between them are either B and C or E and F.

Notice that, in certain sections of the keyboard, the two sets of white keys (B / C and E / F) are closer together than in other sections.

In those sections, notice that there is only one white and two black keys separating the sets (see example below).

Since the letter names of notes (keys) only go from A to G, in succession, then the first set of white keys, at their closest points, would have to be B and C, with the one white key between the two sets being D.

In order for a set of keys to be E and F they would have to be followed by two white keys, G and A, and three black keys, (F ♯ /G ♭) , (G ♯ /A ♭), (A ♯ /B ♭).

All of the letters have to come in alphabetical order:
A B C D E F G.

That's why the *first* set of white keys, at the point where the two sets of white keys are the closest, has to be B and C.

B to C, with D being the next white key; then E to F.

> These are the points where the *two sets* of white keys are closest to each other.

*   *   *

C D E F G A B C D E F G A B C D E F G A B C

3

Notice that each white key has only one letter name and although the black keys have two letter names, they can only be referred to by one of those names at a time, depending upon the *function* the note is required to perform.

If a key is required to be made higher in pitch, it is said to be sharped (♯).

To make a note sharp means to move from that note (key) to a note, or notes, to the right of that note; if <u>one</u> sharp (♯) is required, then move up to the very <u>next</u> key (black or white).

If two sharps are required, then move <u>two</u> keys to the right.

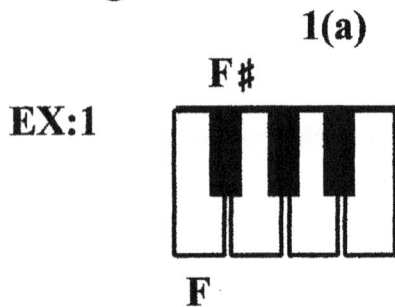

EX:1

1(a) F♯ / F

1(b) B C

Moving from (F) to (F♯) is making the (F) one note sharper, by going to the next key to the right, (F♯).

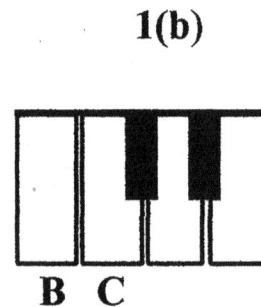

Moving from (B) to (C) is making the (B) one note sharper, by going to the next key to the right, (C).

These are two examples of raising the pitch of a note by one sharp; making the note a *semi-tone* higher.

EX:2

2(a)

F♯ G♯

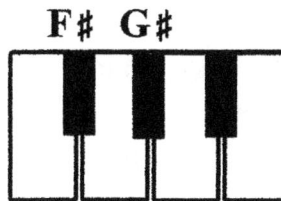

Moving from the (F♯)
to the (G♯) is making
the (F♯) two notes sharper, by
moving two keys to the right (G♯).

2(b)

F   G

Moving from the (F)
to the (G) is making
the (F) two notes sharper, by moving
two keys to the right (G).

These are two examples of raising the pitch of a
note by two sharps ; making the note two *semi-tones* higher,
which is equal to one whole *tone.*

Moving to the right on a keyboard is also referred to as ascending, meaning, moving up.

Moving to the left is referred to as descending, moving down.

If a note is required to be made lower in pitch, it is said to be flatted (♭).

To flat a note means to move from that note (key) to a note, or notes, to the left of that note; if <u>one</u> flat (♭) is required, then move to the very next key (black or white).

If two flats are required, then move <u>two</u> keys to the left.

1(a)   2(a)

EX: 1

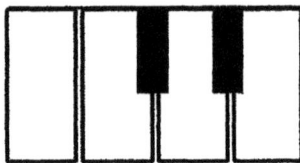

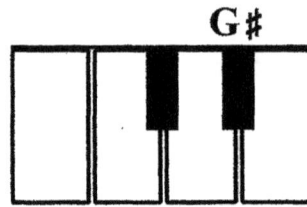

Moving from the (F),
to the (E) is making the (F)
one note flatter, by going
to the next key to the left (E).

Moving from the (G♯) to the
(G) is making the (G♯) one
note flatter, by going to the
next key to the left (G).

These are two examples of lowering the pitch of a note by one flat; making the note a *semi-tone* lower.

2(a)

E♭

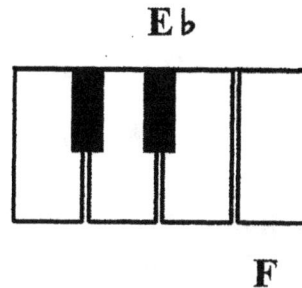

F

Moving from the (F) to the (E♭) is making the (F) two notes flatter, by moving two keys to the left (E♭).

EX: 2

2(b)

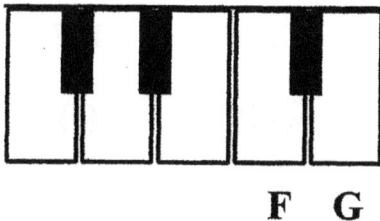

F   G

Moving from the (G) to the (F) is making the (G) two notes flatter, by moving two keys to the left (F).

Above are two examples of lowering the pitch of a note by two flats; making the note two *semi-tones* lower, which is equivalent to one *tone*.

Remember that the *tones* and *semi-tones* are referring to the distances between notes.

<u>Semi-tone</u> = sharping or flatting a note by moving *one* (1) note away from it in *either direction*.

<u>Tone</u> = sharping or flatting a note by moving *two* (2) notes away from it in *either direction*.

<u>FINGERING TIPS</u>

LEFT HAND :	B.F.	R.F.	M.F.	P.F.	T.
	(5)	(4)	(3)	(2)	(1)

B. F. - Baby Finger
R. F. - Ring Finger
M. F. - Middle Finger
P. F. - Pointing Finger
T. - Thumb

RIGHT HAND :	T.	P.F.	M.F.	R.F.	B.F.
	(1)	(2)	(3)	(4)	(5)

DEGREES:	I	II	III	IV	V	VI	VII	VIII
SCALE :	C	D	E	F	G	A	B	C
LEFT HAND	3	2	1	5	4	3	2	1
RIGHT HAND	1	2	3	1	2	3	4	5

   *Roman numerals are sometimes used to number scale degrees and also chords built from a particular scale.
   For instance, a G major chord might be referred to as a V chord in the key of C major.
   You will learn more about chords in the coming chapters.

8

DEGREES:	I	II	III	IV	V	VI	VII	VIII
SCALE :	C	D	E	F	G	A	B	C
LEFT HAND	3	2	1	5	4	3	2	1
RIGHT HAND	1	2	3	1	2	3	4	5

Note that in the left hand fingering, moving from the 1 (thumb) to the 5 (baby finger) seems kind of hard to do.

What we suggest is, crossing *over* the 1 with the 5.

In other words, crossing over the thumb with the baby finger.

If this seems difficult, at first, try playing only to the F note, in order to perfect the crossover.

Also, in the right hand fingering, moving from the 3 (middle finger) to the 1 (thumb) can also present a problem.

What we suggest here is that you cross the thumb *under* the middle finger, in order to reach the F note.

Once again, if it seems difficult, at first, play only to the F note, until you can manage it.

The major scale consists of eight notes. From the starting note (tonic or root note) ascending (moving up) to the same note (tonic) again.

To become a proper major scale, these eight notes must be divided by the correct order of *tones* and *semi-tones* .

The order of *tones* and *semi-tones* (distances between notes) in a major scale are:

Tone-Tone-Semi-tone-Tone-Tone-Tone-Semi-tone

In other words, between the first (1) and second (2) degrees of a major scale there is a distance of a *tone.*

Between the second (2) and third (3) degrees is a *tone.*

Between the third (3) and fourth (4) degrees there is a *semi-tone,* etc.

Below you will find a reference that you can use until you have memorized the proper order of *tones* and *semi-tones* between the degrees of a major scale.

Reference example: 1 2 3 4 5 6 7 8
                    T T S T T T S

Scale of C Major ➜   C D E F G A B C
                     T T S T T T S

Examine the differences between the *tones* and *semi-tones.*

Notice that a *tone* contains a note between two notes, while a *semi-tone* goes directly to the note next to it.

In order to better understand the concept of scales, let's explore, and then complete, the D Major scale.

First we will start with the eight *letters* that are required to form the D Major scale.

D E F G A B C D

These will also be called the degrees of the scale, when they are properly separated according to *tones* and *semi-tones*.

Next let's observe the *tones* and *semi-tones* (distances between the notes) required to put them in the correct order.

Order of *tones & semi-tones*

(DEGREES)	➜	1	2	3	4	5	6	7	8
(DISTANCES)	➜	T	T	S	T	T	T	S	

Now let's separate the degrees according to the proper *tones* and *semi-tones* as shown above.

EXAMPLE:

From   the   scale   of   D   Major

D to D♯ = 1 *semi-tone* ➜
+
<u>D♯ to   E = 1 *semi-tone* ➜</u>

D to D♯ to E = 1 *tone*

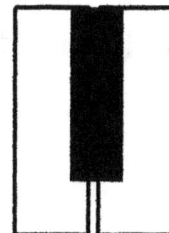

D   E

Since a *tone* consists of **2** *semi-tones*, and we have covered the distance of **2** *semi-tones* from D to E; we can safely say that the distance between D and E is a *tone* (*semitone + semitone = tone*).

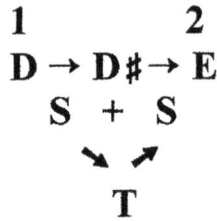

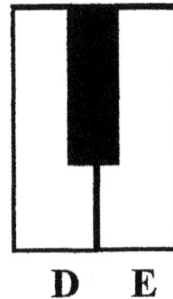

A *tone* is also required between the second (2) and third (3) degrees of a major scale.

With the second (2) degree being E and the third (3) degree being F and by observing the notes on the piano, we find that a correction needs to be made because E goes directly to F, making them only a *semitone* apart, when a *tone* is needed.

Since from E to F is only a *semi-tone*, another *semi-tone* is required. In order to put a *tone* between the second (2) and third (3) degrees, it is required that we change F to F♯, adding another *semi-tone*.

Now we have the first three degrees of the D Major scale as follows:

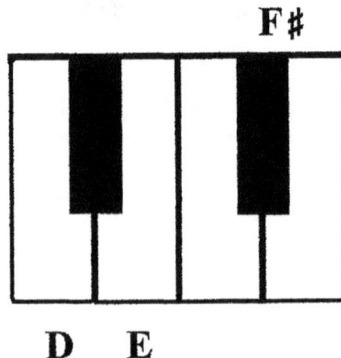

The next step requires that we put a *semi-tone* between the third (3) and fourth (4) degrees of the major scale.

With the third (3) degree being F♯, we know that the fourth (4) degree is required to be a *semi-tone* above F♯, where we find G, exactly a *semi-tone* above.

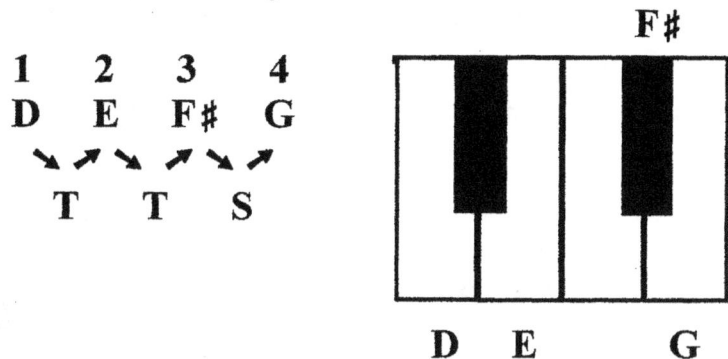

Continuing to form a major scale, in the key of D, let's proceed to the fifth (5) degree.

Referring back to the correct order of *tones* and *semi-tones* that constitute a major scale, we find that between the fourth (4) and fifth (5) degrees of the scale, the distance of a *tone* is required.

EXAMPLE: 1 2 3 4 5 6 7 8
                T T S T T T S

Knowing that from G is G♯ is only a *semi-tone*, we find that in order to complete the distance of a *tone* we must add another *semi-tone*, thus moving from G *through* G♯ to A.

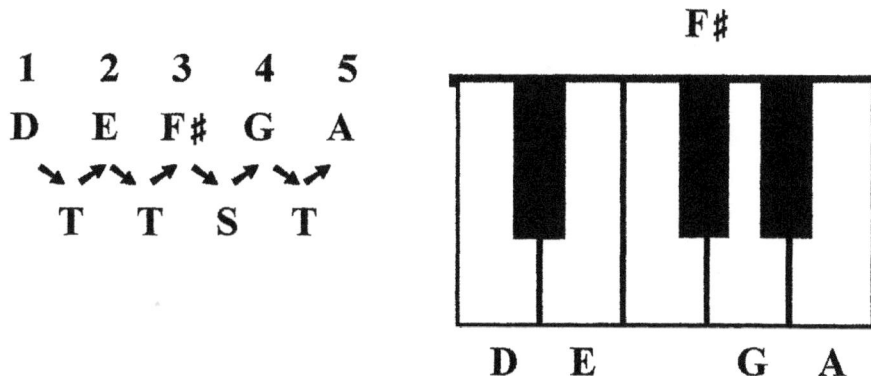

Proceeding from the fifth (5) to the sixth (6) degree, we notice that another *tone* is required between the two.

In order to achieve this, we must start at A, pass through A♯ (covering a *semitone*), then move from A♯ to B (covering another *semi-tone*), thus completing the distance of a *tone*.

This gives us the first 6 degrees of the D Major scale.

```
1   2   3   4   5   6
D   E   F♯  G   A   B
  ↘↗  ↘↗  ↘↗  ↘  ↗↘  ↗
   T   T   S   T   T
```

From the sixth (6) to the seventh (7) degree, a *tone* is also required.

As you will see, when looking at the notes on a piano, from B to C is the distance of a *semi-tone*.

Since B to C is only a *semi-tone*, we shall proceed from B on to C#, in order to create a *tone* between the sixth (6) and seventh (7) degrees of the D Major scale.

1	2	3	4	5	6	7
D	E	F#	G	A	B	C#

T   T   S   T   T   T

As we approach the end of the D Major scale, we see from our reference example, that a *semi-tone* is required between the seventh (7) and eighth (8) degrees of a major scale.

Starting from the seventh (7) degree [C♯] of the D Major scale, we move directly to the eighth (8) degree [D], which is the required *semi-tone* between the last two notes (degrees) of the major scale.

```
1    2    3    4    5    6    7    8
D    E    F♯   G    A    B    C♯   D
  ↘↗  ↘↗  ↘↗  ↘↗  ↘↗  ↘↗  ↘↗
  T    T    S    T    T    T    S
```

```
D    E       G    A    B       D
```

While playing the scale of D Major; (D E F♯ G A B C♯ D) you may notice that it is in the *melody*, or the *tune* of, Do Re Mi Fa So La Ti Do.

This is also the case with *every* properly constructed major scale; they will always be in the exact melody of Do Re Mi Fa So La Ti Do, only in different pitches (higher or lower in sound).

16

Although each major scale is different in appearance from the others, they are all formed, and governed, by the same principle (T T S T T T S) separating the degrees.
EXAMPLES:

C Major scale

C D E F G A B C
  T T S T T T S

B Major scale

B C# D# E F# G# A# B
  T T S T T T S

A Major scale

A B C# D E F# G# A
  T T S T T T S

E Major scale

E F# G# A B C# D# E
  T T S T T T S

G Major scale

G A B C D E F# G
  T T S T T T S

You may have noticed that the scale (or key) of <u>C Major</u> contains no sharps (♯) or flats (♭).

This is because the *tones* and *semi-tones* line up perfectly, without the need of sharps or flats.

You may have also noticed that, up until this point, we haven't created a major scale containing any flats (♭).

To begin learning about the need for using flats in a major scale, let's begin with an <u>F Major scale</u>.

We begin with the necessary *letters*:

F G A B C D E F

Since we know that all major scales are formed using the (T T S T T T S) theory, let's begin creating an <u>F Major scale</u>.

EXAMPLE: 1   2   3   4
           F   G   A   B
             T   T   T

Observing the above example, we find that the order of *tones* and *semi-tones* is correct only up to the third (3) degree, which is the A note.

Between the third (3) <u>A</u> and fourth (4) <u>B</u> degrees, a *semi-tone* is required.

Since there is already a *tone* between A and B, and only a *semi-tone* is needed, adding a sharp to A would put the third (3) and fourth (4) degrees a *semi-tone* apart; but it would then create a *tone* + a *semi-tone* (*tone* ½) between the second (2) and third (3) degrees.

EXAMPLE: 1   2   3   4
           F G A♯   B
             T T½ S

In order to create a *semi-tone* between the third (3) and fourth (4) degrees, we simply move the fourth (4) degree , B, down (descending; *to the left*) by a *semi-tone*.

EXAMPLE: 1   2   3   4
F   G   A   B♭
T   T   S

After completing the <u>F Major scale</u> we will find that all of the other degrees of the scale line up naturally, without the need for alterations.

EXAMPLE: 1   2   3   4   5   6   7   8
F   G   A   B♭   C   D   E   F
T   T   S   T   T   T   S

If you haven't already figured it out, let's see why the black keys have two names.
We will begin by comparing two notes in the <u>B Major scale</u> and <u>F Major scale</u>

B C♯ D♯ E F♯ G♯ A♯   B
                                ↕
       F   G   A   B♭ C   D   E   F

Although these two notes (A♯ and B♭) are called by two different names, they are indeed, found on the very same black key. They are named according to what their functions (*jobs*) are in their respective scales.
A♯ is needed to make a note higher in pitch and B♭ is needed to make a note lower in pitch.

Another area of the major scales that requires some special attention is the major scales that have sharp (♯) or flat (♭) beginning (root) notes.

EXAMPLE:

<u>**F♯ Major scale**</u>

1	2	3	4	5	6	7	8
F♯	G♯	A♯	B	C♯	D♯	E♯	F♯
	T	T	S	T	T	T	S

Examining the notes of the keyboard, you will find that there is no B♯, C♭, E♯, F♭, to be found.

Yet in the <u>F♯ Major scale</u>, we find an E♯; this is because when writing a major scale, *all of the degrees have to have a different letter name* [except the eighth (8) degree which is the same as the first (1) degree].

Actually, E♯ is F, because F is the *semi-tone* or next note up from E, making the E sharp.

EXAMPLE:

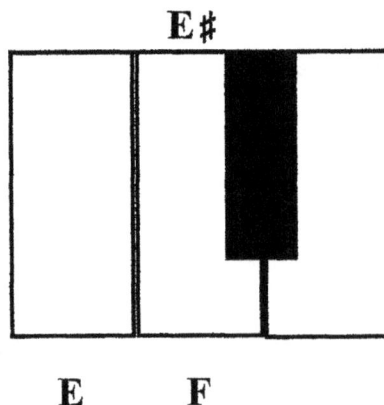

Now let's look at a scale using a C♭.

EXAMPLE:

G♭ Major scale

1	2	3	4	5	6	7	8
G♭	A♭	B♭	C♭	D♭	E♭	F	G♭
	T	T	S	T	T	T	S

As you can see, the fourth (4) degree is a C♭ and there is no such note on the keyboard.

The note called a C♭ is really a B, but because we cannot have a scale with B♭ and B (*each note has to have a different letter name*), we call the fourth (4) degree C♭.

*Remember every major scale, before the *tones* and *semi-tones* are applied, starts out with the seven *different letter* names, beginning and ending with the root (1) and (8) note, *which is the root note repeated.*

Also keep in mind that the only letters used are A B C D E F G.

There is no alphabet in music above G. After G, we go back to A.

Let's now look at the <u>C# Major scale</u>

EXAMPLE:

1	2	3	4	5	6	7	8
C#	D#	E#	F#	G#	A#	B#	C#
	T	T	S	T	T	T	S

The third (3) degree, [E#], is actually [F], creating a *semi-tone* between the third (3) and fourth (4) degrees; the seventh (7) degree, [B#], is actually [C], creating a *semi-tone* between the seventh (7) and eighth (8) degrees.

Learn to recognize notes such as these, so that you won't be confused between what you are seeing and what you are supposed to play.

*Remember:

$$B\# = C \qquad C\flat = B \qquad E\# = F \qquad F\flat = E$$

Because of key signatures (for explanation turn to Chapter 9) it is sometimes necessary for one scale name to defer to another.

I will explain: In a key signature there is a limit to the amount of (#'s) or (♭'s) that are allowed.

That limit is 7 (#'s) and 7 (♭'s), but there are some scales that would exceed the limit.

Examining the key (scale) of D♯ Major, we find that it contains *two* degrees, (3) and (7), that have double sharps (♯♯).

EXAMPLE:

1	2	3	4	5	6	7	8
D♯	E♯	F♯♯	G♯	A♯	B♯	C♯♯	D♯

By looking at the above example, you can count and see that you would exceed the maximum number of (♯'s) or (♭'s) allowed in a key signature, which is seven each.

So, as we previously stated, this is where one scale name would have to give in (defer) to the other.

Instead of being called D♯ Major, this scale would be called, and written as E♭ Major.

Here's why:

1	2	3	4	5	6	7	8
D♯	E♯	F♯♯	G♯	A♯	B♯	C♯♯	D♯
↕	↕	↕	↕	↕	↕	↕	↕
1	2	3	4	5	6	7	8
E♭	F	G	A♭	B♭	C	D	E♭

The notes in each scale are identical, although called by different names (compare them on the keyboard); but E♭ Major has only 3 (♭'s), (*you wouldn't count the one on the eighth (8) degree because it is a repeat*), and D♯ Major has 9 (♯'s) !!

Since the 3 (♭'s) in E♭ Major fall within the allowed number for the key signature (7), the D♯ Major scale would defer to the E♭ Major scale, meaning that the E♭ Major scale would win out as the choice of what key signature to write.

This is a rule that you should keep in mind: While constructing a major scale, if you come across double (##'s) or double (♭♭'s), the key signature will be the opposite of the one with the doubles.

EXAMPLES:

G#	A#	B#	C#	D#	E#	F##	G#
↕	↕	↕	↕	↕	↕	↕	↕
A♭	B♭	C	D♭	E♭	F	G	A♭

The A♭ Major scale is parallel to the G# Major scale because all of the notes sound the same, the only difference is, they have different *letter* names.

The key signature though, will obviously be in A♭ Major because G# Major has one too many (#'s). [*Do not count the (#) or (♭) on the eighth (8) degree because it is a repeat of the first (1) degree*].

Let's look at another example and figure out which scale the key signature would be named for.

EXAMPLES:

A#	B#	C##	D#	E#	F##	G##	A#
↕	↕	↕	↕	↕	↕	↕	↕
B♭	C	D	E♭	F	G	A	B♭

With 10 (#'s) in the key of A# Major, which exceeds the limit, the choice would obviously be B♭ Major with 2 (♭'s).

This is a list of all of the major scales that have a key signature. Any other major scale would be a *synonym* to one of these scales.

In other words, they would contain the same notes as one of these scales, but with different *letter* names.
EXAMPLES:

			Scale					Key Signature
C	D	E	F	G	A	B	C	0 (♯'s) or (♭'s)
G	A	B	C	D	E	F♯	G	1 (♯)
D	E	F♯	G	A	B	C♯	D	2 (♯'s)
A	B	C♯	D	E	F♯	G♯	A	3 (♯'s)
E	F♯	G♯	A	B	C♯	D♯	E	4 (♯'s)
B	C♯	D♯	E	F♯	G♯	A♯	B	5 (♯'s)
F♯	G♯	A♯	B	C♯	D♯	E♯	F♯	6 (♯'s)
C♯	D♯	E♯	F♯	G♯	A♯	B♯	C♯	7 (♯'s)
F	G	A	B♭	C	D	E	F	1 (♭)
B♭	C	D	E♭	F	G	A	B♭	2 (♭'s)
E♭	F	G	A♭	B♭	C	D	E♭	3 (♭'s)
A♭	B♭	C	D♭	E♭	F	G	A♭	4 (♭'s)
D♭	E♭	F	G♭	A♭	B♭	C	D♭	5 (♭'s)
G♭	A♭	B♭	C♭	D♭	E♭	F	G♭	6 (♭'s)
C♭	D♭	E♭	F♭	G♭	A♭	B♭	C♭	7 (♭'s)

* If you are interested in learning about key signatures, at this point, then turn to the section on <u>Understanding Key Signatures</u>.

FINGERING FOR CHORDS

For playing chords, we can use either of two types of fingering.

First, there is what we call the closed chord fingering.

EXAMPLE :

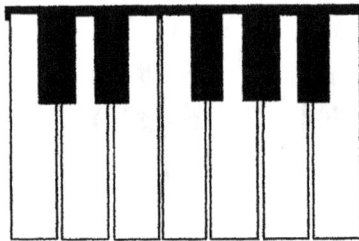

	C	E	G
R.H.	1	3	5
L.H.	5	3	1

The reason that we call these fingerings closed is because of the tight positioning of the fingers.

We recommend this type of fingering when there are melody notes to be played between chords that are located in the same register (area) of the keyboard as the chords.

For instance, if the D note in the example above, needed to be played, the 2 finger (R.H.) or the 4 finger (L.H.) would already be in position to play it.

This is what we call the open chord fingering style.

EXAMPLE :

C major 7

	C	E	G	B
R.H.	1	2	3	4
L.H.	4	3	2	1

The reason that we call these fingerings open is because of the fingers being stretched out.

Also, this is the positioning that we recommend for playing extension chords (4 or more notes), for obvious reasons.

As you can see, playing extension chords would be impossible in the closed fingering position, without using two hands.

Experiment to find which fingerings work best for you, in different situations.

Since there are many different ways to play melodies *and* chords, consider these as helpful suggestions.

Chapter 2

Chords

Now that we have learned about *tones* and *semi-tones*, the degrees of a major scale, sharps and flats, and how they come together to form a major scale; let's explore the major scale even further.

From a properly constructed major scale, we can extract (or take) *chords*.

A chord is when three (3) or more notes are played simultaneously (at the same time).

There is a system that allows us to form chords using every degree of a major scale, as a root (starting) note; we call it the *take one, skip one, take one, skip one, take one* method.

Let's see how it works; by forming triads (three note chords) using the <u>C Major scale.</u>

EXAMPLE:

①	2	3	4	5	6	7	8
C	D	E	F	G	A	B	C
↕		↕		↕			
C		E		G			
❶		❸		❺			

C   E   G

By using the *take one, skip one, take one, skip one, take one* method, we have just formed our first triad (three note chord) using the first (1) degree from the <u>C Major scale</u>, as our root note.

The notes are C E G; the chord is called a C major chord . It is called a C chord because the root (beginning) note is a C.

When we reach the section on <u>Classifying Chords</u> we will learn why it is called major.

Let's continue to use *the take one, skip one, take one, skip one, take one* method to build triads (three note chords) from the <u>C Major scale</u>, by using the second (2) degree as our root (starting) note.

EXAMPLE:

1	②	3	4	5	6	7	8
C	D	E	F	G	A	B	C
	↕		↕		↕		
	D		F		A		
	❶		❸		❺		

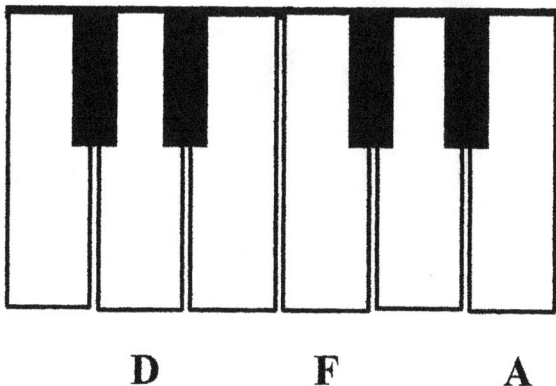

D   F   A

The triad built from the second (2) degree of the C Major scale contains the notes D F A, and is called a D minor chord.

As with the C Major chord, it is called a D chord because the root is a D.

It is called minor for reasons that we will discuss in the Classifying Chords section.

Continuing to use the *take one, skip one, take one, skip one, take one* (ta-ski-ta-ski-ta) method, let's form a chord using the third (3) degree of the C Major scale as our root note.

EXAMPLE:

1	2	③	4	5	6	7	8
C	D	E	F	G	A	B	C
		↕		↕		↕	
		E		G		B	
		❶		❸		❺	

The numbers circled in black represent the root position (1-3-5) of the chord; which we will study in a coming chapter.

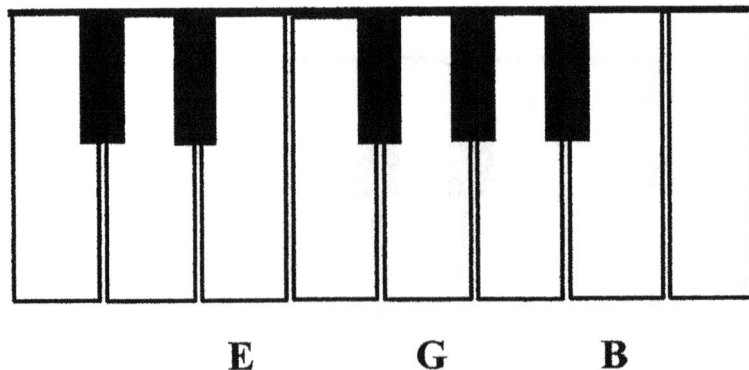

E   G   B

The triad built from the third (3) degree of the C Major scale contains the notes E G B, and is called an E minor chord.

Let's proceed to build a triad using the fourth (4) degree of the C Major scale as our root note.

EXAMPLE:

1	2	3	④	5	6	7	8
C	D	E	F	G	A	B	C
			↕		↕		↕
			F		A		C
			❶		❸		❺

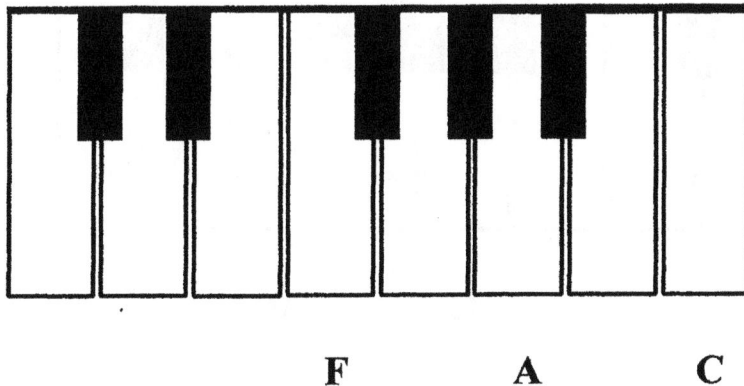

F   A   C

Built from the fourth (4) degree of the C Major scale, containing the notes, F A C, we now have an F major chord.

Starting on the fifth (5) degree, let's build the next chord (triad).

EXAMPLE:

1	2	3	4	⑤	6	7	8	9
C	D	E	F	G	A	B	C	D
				↕		↕		↕
				G		B		D
				❶		❸		❺

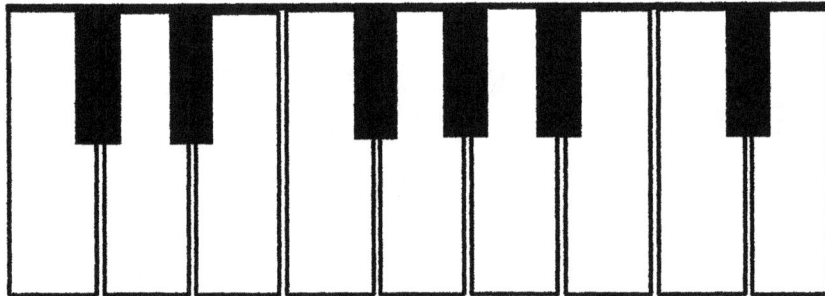

G   B   D

Although the D note is taken from the ninth (9) degree of the scale, it still holds the position of being the (5) note of the chord, as in (1-3-5).

In actuality there are only 8 degrees in a major scale, but for the purpose of forming triads *(in root position)* using the 5th, 6th, or 7th degrees as starting notes, or forming *some* extension chords *in root position* it is necessary to continue to keep moving up the keyboard.

The notes built from the fifth (5) degree of C Major are G B D, in that order.

This chord is called G major.

Let's build the chord that uses the sixth (6) degree as it's root note.

EXAMPLE:

1	2	3	4	5	⑥	7	8	9	10
C	D	E	F	G	A	B	C	D	E
					↕		↕		↕
					A		C		E
					❶		❸		❺

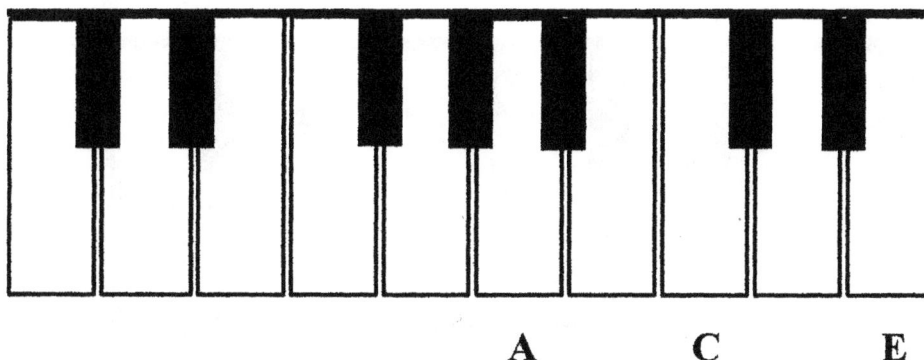

            A   C   E

Again, because of the natural progression, D comes after C and E comes after D, using the (ta-ski-ta-ski-ta) method, we move up to the E note, which is our last note in the chord, in the root position (1,3,5).

The notes built from the sixth (6) degree are A C E, in that order.

The chord is called an A minor. [*Begin to notice the difference in sounds; between the major and minor chords*]

Now we shall build the last chord in the
C Major scale , using the seventh (7) degree as it's root.

EXAMPLE:

1	2	3	4	5	6	⑦	8	9	10	11
C	D	E	F	G	A	B	C	D	E	F
						↕		↕		↕
						B		D		F
						❶		❸		❺

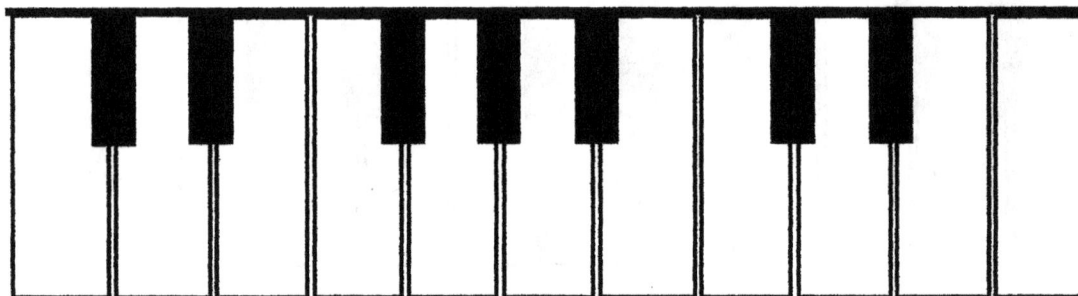

B   D   F

The name of this chord, containing the notes,
B D F, in that order, is B diminished.

Notice that the sound of the diminished chord is different from a major *and* a minor chord.

The diminished chord creates a feeling of suspense or incompleteness.

Let's revisit all of the chords (triads) contained in the <u>C Major scale</u>.

EXAMPLE:

<u>Degrees</u>	<u>Chords</u>	<u>Type</u>	<u>Symbol</u>
1	C E G	Major	C (or) CM
2	D F A	minor	Dm
3	E G B	minor	Em
4	F A C	Major	F (or) FM
5	G B D	Major	G (or) GM
6	A C E	minor	Am
7	B D F	diminished	B^o

* NOTE: Major chords are often referred to by the root name only (without the M sign); so it is assumed that when a chord is represented by only the one letter name, the chord is major. Minor and diminished chords are always referred to and written as, minor (m) or diminished (o) or dim.

All of the rules and principles that we have used to form chords from the <u>C Major scale</u> are the same ones used to form chords *in all of the major scales.*

When major scales are properly formed, according to the distances of *(tones & semi-tones),* they yield the same chord types on each respective degree of the scale.

EXAMPLE:

1	=	Major
2	=	minor
3	=	minor
4	=	Major
5	=	Major
6	=	minor
7	=	diminished

Once you have learned how all of these principles work in one key *(scale),* you can apply them to every major scale.

For instance, in every major scale, the first (1) chord will be a major chord. The second (2) chord will be a minor chord etc. (see example above).

You should also be able to look at a major scale and pick out the chords, using *the ta-ski-ta-ski-ta method.*

Here is the D major scale and it's respective chords. (*you'll find every major scale and their chords in Chapter 10*)

<u>D Major scale</u>

1	2	3	4	5	6	7	8
D	E	F♯	G	A	B	C♯	D

<u>Chords in D Major</u>

1 = D F♯ A = D

2 = E G B = Em

3 = F♯ A C♯ = F♯m

4 = G B D = G

5 = A C♯ E = A

6 = B D F♯ = Bm

7 = C♯ E G = C♯^{o}

Chapter 3

Classifying   Chords

Classifying chords requires a complete understanding of how a major scale is constructed.

The reason for this is that every triad (*3 note chord*) taken from a major scale, using the *ta-ski-ta-ski-ta* method, has to be compared to the (1),(3), and (5) notes of the major scale having the *same root note* as the particular chord.

EXAMPLE:

The chord C E G has to be compared to the (1), (3), and (5)   notes of the <u>C Major scale.</u>

If, when comparing the chord against the scale, the (1), (3), and (5) line up exactly, then the chord is classified as a <u>major chord</u>. C E G is a C major chord.

EXAMPLE:

<u>C Major scale (first five notes)</u>

```
          ①   2   3   4   5
          C   D   E   F   G
          ↕       ↕       ↕
Chord →   C       E       G
          ❶       ❸       ❺
```

* The first chord taken from a major scale will naturally match up exactly because it is being taken from itself. So the first (1) chord will always be a *major chord*.

Since, as we have learned, the chord built from the (2) degree is a minor chord, let's find out why.

In order to classify a chord, remember that the notes of the chord have to be compared to the (1), (3), and (5) notes of the major scale with the same root (1) note as the chord.

Staying in the C Major scale (C D E F G A B C), let's classify the chord built on the (2) degree [D], using the *ta-ski-ta-ski-ta* method.

EXAMPLE:

	❶	♭❸		❺	
Chord ➡	D	F		A	
	↕	↕		↕	
D Major scale ➡	D	E	F♯	G	A	(first 5 notes)
	①	2	3	4	5	

Notice that the notes which we are using for a comparison are the (1), (3), and (5) notes of the D Major scale, although the *chord* comes from the C Major scale.

The reason is that the root (1) note of the chord is D, thus the comparison to the D Major scale.

Remember that in order to classify a chord, it has to be compared to the identical degrees (notes) of the major scale with the same (1) root note as the chord.

The above chord, D F A, is a D minor chord; on the next page we will find out why.

The three types of triads (3 note chords) that are yielded from a major scale are: major, minor, and diminished.

As previously stated, when comparing the notes of a chord to the same degrees (notes) of it's respective (same root note) major scale, if the (1),(3), and (5) degrees match perfectly between chord and scale, then the chord is major.

The formula for a major chord is 1 - 3 - 5, meaning that, the chord takes the (1),(3), and (5) degrees from the major scale with the *same name* .

The formula for a minor chord is 1 - ♭3 - 5, meaning that, when comparing the notes of the chord to the notes of it's respective major scale (*same root notes*), the third (3) degree of the [*chord*] is a *semi-tone* lower than the third (3) degree of the [*scale*].

EXAMPLE:

	❶	**♭❸**		**❺**	
Chord ➡	A	C		E	
	↕	↕		↕	
A Major scale ➡	A	B	C♯ D	E	(first 5 notes)
	①	2	3 4	5	

As you can see, the C note in the chord is a *semi-tone* lower than the C♯ note in the scale. The (1) and the (5) degrees match perfectly in both the chord and the scale, thus the 1 - ♭3 - 5.

The formula for a diminished chord is 1-♭3-♭5, meaning that, when comparing the notes of the chord to the notes of it's respective major scale (*same root note*), the third (3) degree and the (5) degree of the [*chord*] are each a *semi-tone* lower than the third (3) degree and the (5) degree of the [*scale*].

In the key (scale) of <u>C Major</u>, the chord built from the seventh (7) degree, B D F, is a diminished chord.

EXAMPLE:

	❶		♭❸		♭❺	
Chord ➜	B		D		F	
B Major scale ➜	B	C♯	D♯	E	F♯	(first 5 notes)
	①	2	3	4	5	

In *every* major scale, the chord that is built from the seventh (7) degree is a diminished chord.

There is another type of triad (3 note chord) that is *not* found in a major scale. It is called an augmented chord.

To augment, means to embellish or to add something to; in this case we are embellishing the third (3) and fifth (5) degrees.

EXAMPLE:

	❶		♯❸		♯❺	
Chord ➜	B		D♯♯ (E)		F♯♯ (G)	
B Major scale ➜	B	C♯	D♯	E	F♯	(first 5 notes)
	①	2	3	4	5	

Since the 3rd & 5th notes were already sharp; adding another sharp made them double sharp, often indicated by (x).

From the example, we can observe that by taking a major chord (1, 3, 5) and raising the 3rd and 5th notes by a *semi-tone*, it becomes an augmented chord.

The formula for an augmented chord is 1 - #3 - #5, meaning that, when comparing the notes of the chord to the notes of it's respective (*same root note*) major scale, the (3) and (5) notes are a *semi-tone* higher in the chord than they were in the major scale.

There is another type of triad, a suspended 4th, that is formed by playing the 1-4-5 degrees of a major scale.

These different classifications of chords are sometimes referred to as chord colors, for obvious reasons.

Study these chapters on scales, the chords that each particular scale yields, and how to classify chords, very closely and often because they are the foundation for music in the major scale.

Chapter 4

<u>Chord   Functions</u>

In every major scale each chord has a function, or
a certain job to do, according to the degree upon which it
falls.

Although the chords vary by name and pitch, each
has the same function from scale to scale, depending upon
the degree on which each chord falls.

For instance, in the scale of <u>D Major,</u> the chord
formed on the fourth (4) degree is G (or GM).

In the scale of <u>C Major</u> the chord formed on the
fourth (4) degree is F (or FM).

Even though these two chords [G and F] are
different in pitch, they each have the same function or
purpose, in their respective scales.

There are three categories or functions that the
chords of a major scale are divided into; and they are the
<u>Tonic</u>, <u>Subdominant</u>, or <u>Dominant</u> .

EXAMPLE:

<u>Tonic</u>	<u>Subdominant</u>	<u>Dominant</u>
(1) (3) (6)	(2) (4)	(5) (7)

*The above example is the formula for chord functions
in every major scale, please memorize it.*

Chords built upon each of the degrees above will
have the same *function* in *every* major scale.

The (1), (3), and (6) degrees will always belong to the
<u>Tonic</u> function, the (2) and (4) degrees will always belong to
the <u>Subdominant</u> function, and the (5) and (7) degrees will
always belong to the <u>Dominant</u> function.

43

As you can see, every chord of the major scale comes under one of the categories (<u>Tonic</u>, <u>Subdominant</u>, or <u>Dominant</u>).

Notice that chords with *different classifications* (major, minor, or diminished) can have the same *function*.

EXAMPLE:
<u>Tonic</u>
(1) Major (3) minor (6) minor

Let's look further into the meaning of chord functions.

The function of a <u>Tonic</u> chord is to be the primary (or main) sound that all of the other chords revolve around and come back to.

Generally, in a piece of music, the <u>Tonic</u> chords are played more often than any other, giving the music a sense of grounding or centering it.

A piece of music *usually* begins and ends with a <u>Tonic</u> chord, helping to define the tonality (key or scale).

Moving from one chord to another chord within the same function group *can* sound uneventful; that is because they serve the same purpose in the scale.

EXAMPLE:
<u>Key of C Major</u>

C   Am
/ / / /   / / / /
count ➔ 1 2 3 4   1 2 3 4

In the key of <u>C Major</u>, playing from C to Am is allowed, but there is not much of a change taking place from (1) tonic to (6) tonic).

This is where the need for <u>Subdominant</u> and <u>Dominant</u> chords comes in, to provide some contrast and a release.

The function of the <u>Subdominant</u> (sometimes called passing) chords is mainly to provide a change from the <u>Tonic</u> chords, coloring and making the music more interesting, in the process.

Although the following example is in the key of <u>C Major</u>, the functions of the chords on each respective degree are the same in every major scale.

EXAMPLE:

<u>Key of C Major</u>

(6)	(4)	(6)	(5) (7)
Am	F	Am	G Bdim
/ / / /	/ / / /	/ / / /	/ / / /
TONIC	S.DOM	TONIC	DOM. - DOM.

Notice the slight change between Am and F, but the more pronounced change between Am and G. Also notice that in the G to B(dim.) change, the seven chord [B dim.] is giving the five chord [G] a slight lift, although they both have the same function.

However, listen carefully as you play this progression, and you will hear that ending on a <u>Dominant</u> chord leaves an unresolved or unfinished sound.

This is because a <u>Dominant</u> chord usually leads back to a <u>Tonic</u> chord, either directly, or by moving to a <u>Sub - dominant</u> chord and then to a <u>Tonic</u> chord, for a completed or resolved sound.

When looking to make a noticeable change in a *chord progression* (chords played in succession), a chord from the <u>Dominant</u> group will most likely be the best choice.

A Dominant chord is called a turnaround chord because of the need to go back to the Tonic chord.

<u>EXAMPLE</u>
<u>Key of C major</u>

Bdim   **C**
/ / / /   / / / /

Notice that the Bdim chord sounds incomplete until you play the C chord. This is called *resolving* the Dominant (Bdim) chord to the Tonic (C) chord.

* Think of a Sub-dominant chord, as coloring; being used to bridge the gap between Tonic to Tonic chords and to bridge Tonic to Dominant chords or Dominant back to Tonic chords.

EXAMPLE

Key of C major

C	Dm	Em
/ / / /	/ / / /	/ / / /

In this example, you could actually move from C directly to Em and it would sound fine, but inserting the Dm makes the transition more interesting.

When moving from a Tonic chord to a Sub-dominant chord, the closer the two chords are together, the smoother the transition will be.

In other words, if you start with a C (Tonic) and move to the Dm (Sub-dominant) right next to the C, it would sound smoother than if you started with a C (Tonic) and moved to the F (Sub-dominant) 2 ½ tones to the right of C, because the first two chords are closer in proximity (closer together).

Because musical tastes vary, you might not always want a smooth transition, so experiment and decide which way *you* want to go.

Remember, the more you know about music, the more you will be able to express yourself musically.

My intention is to help you to arrive at a place of complete musical freedom, so please study HARD.

47

EXAMPLE
Key of C major

C	F	G	Dm	C
/ / / /	/ / / /	/ / / /	/ / / /	/ / / /

This example is showing how to bridge a *Tonic* chord to a *Dominant* chord and a *Dominant* chord back to a *Tonic* chord, as discussed on the previous page.

In this case, for the 2nd chord, we used the *Sub - dominant (4)* chord (F), instead of the *Sub - dominant (2)* chord (Dm), to bridge the *Tonic (1)* chord (C) to the *Dominant (5)* chord (G).

For variation, moving back from the *Dominant (5)* chord (G) we use a *Sub - dominant (2)* chord (Dm).

Try reversing the F chord and the Dm chord, to hear what effect it will have, since they are both *Sub - dominant* chords.

EXAMPLE
Key of C major

C	Dm	G	F	C
/ / / /	/ / / /	/ / / /	/ / / /	/ / / /

As you can hear, it is all a matter of what you are trying to achieve.

They are both right, but you will make these choices according to your personal tastes

That is the point to studying music, to be able to express *yourself.*

Here is another way to connect *Tonic* to *Dominant* chords, by way of passing *(Sub - dominant)* chords.

<u>EXAMPLE</u>
<u>Key of C major</u>

C   Dm   C   F G   C
/ / / /   / / / /   / / / /   / / / /   / / / /

Even though the previous examples were in the key of C major, the above example has more of a sense of being in C major because of the more frequent use of the C major chord.

Also, notice how the F chord and G chord only last for two beats each, wasting no time in getting back to the *Tonic.*

Chapter 5

Chord Inversions

Something else that you will need to be aware of when creating chord progressions is *chord inversions* and *extension chords*.

Chord inversions can often help to bring a completely fresh sound to regular sounding chords.

To invert something means to turn it around; inverting a chord means to do the same thing, to put the notes in a different order.

There are two types of inversions, first inversion and second inversion.

The following is an example of the first inversion of an A major chord.

EXAMPLE:

Key of A Major

1	3	5	
A	C♯	E	← root position

C♯	E	A	
3	5	1	← first inversion

In this example, by moving the root (1) up an octave, the chord becomes inverted in the first position.

Any triad with the notes played in this order, (3), (5), (1) is in the *first inversion* position.

Any triad using the (1), (3), (5) order of the notes is called the *root position*, because that is the original position in which the chord was formed.

The second inversion position is when the notes are placed in the (5), (1), (3) order, placing the (1) and the (3) an octave up from their original positions.

Notice that each time a chord is inverted, the bottom note is being moved up an octave, so the second inversion of a chord is actually the natural next step after the first inversion.

EXAMPLE:

<u>**Key of A Major**</u>

1	3	5	
A	C♯	E	← root position
3	5	1	
C♯	E	A	← first inversion
5	1	3	
E	A	C♯	← second inversion

Although a *triad* can be played in a fourth position (A E C), we do not recommend it, unless you're looking for a more open or spatial sound.

Try experimenting by inverting different chords to hear what the changes sound like (playing some chords in root position; along with other chords using the first or second inversions)

Also try to combine different chord types (major, minor, diminished, and augmented) to add contrast.

Chapter 6

Extension   Chords

Extension chords, chords with four or more different notes, can be very helpful in making a piece of music more interesting, in various ways.

These chords can be played along with triads (three note chords) or completely by themselves, giving the music a broader sound.

Let's find out how they are formed, what their chord functions are, how they are classified, and some ways to apply them.

We will begin with a major sixth chord, because the 6th chord is the first in the line of extension chords, using the symbol (M6).

The formula for a major 6th chord is 1 -3 -5 -6.

EXAMPLE:

Key of C Major

	❶		❸		❺	❻
Chord →	C		E		G	A
	C	D	E	F	G	A
	①	2	3	4	5	6

The preceding example is a C major 6th or most often called a C 6.

A major 6th chord, as the name implies, is classified as major, and usually functions as part of whatever category of chords it belonged to in the first place, relevant to the scale from which it was taken.

Anytime the 6th note of the scale from which a *major triad* is taken, is added to that triad, it becomes a major 6th or a 6th chord.

The next four-note chord that we will look at is the major 7th chord.

The formula for a major 7th chord is 1-3-5-7, leaving every degree of the chord the same as they are in the corresponding major scale.

EXAMPLE:

❶		❸		❺		❼	
C		E		G		B	

C	D	E	F	G	A	B	C
①	2	3	4	5	6	7	8

Under normal circumstances, playing two notes (*at the same time*) which are only a *semi-tone* apart, would create a dissonant or unpleasant sound.

I am referring to the (7) B and the (8) C, but in this case we don't have to worry about that because the root [C] is being played on the (1) degree, which is far enough away from the (7) B to not cause any dissonance.

If you were to invert this CM7 chord (first inversion), by putting the root on top, it would sound pretty bad.

Try playing it for yourself and you'll hear what I mean.

The reason that this move doesn't sound good, is that the two notes that are a *semi-tone* apart are now being played in close proximity; (7) B and (8)C.

As long as the two notes were being played at opposite ends of the chord, they worked fine, but placing them side by side creates a clash.

EXAMPLE:

❸	❺	❼	❽
E	G	B	C

C	D	E	F	G	A	B	C
1	2	3	4	5	6	7	8

These notes, E, G, B, and C, are all of the notes of a CM7 chord, but playing them in this particular order will definitely create a dissonant sound.

From this observation we have determined that a major 7th chord should *not* be played using the root next to the 7th.

Let's now examine the *dominant* seventh chord, created by adding a flatted seventh note to a major triad (1,3,5 chord).

EXAMPLE:

1	3		5	♭7			
F	A		C	E♭			
↕	↕		↕	↕			
F	G	A	B♭	C	D	E	F
①	2	3	4	5	6	7	8

The formula for a dominant seventh chord is 1 - 3 - 5 - ♭7; written as the root note followed by a 7. (Example above F 7).

The dominant seventh chord, as the name implies, belongs to the dominant function group.

However, the more chord knowledge that a person acquires, the way in which they apply it becomes a matter of personal taste.

The next chord that we will examine in the progression of extension chords is the dominant ninth chord, which also belongs to the dominant function group, as the name implies.

The formula for the ninth chord is $1 - 3 - 5 - b7 - 9$, with the (9) actually being the (2), only up an octave.

EXAMPLE:

		*		
1	3	5	b7	9
A	C#	E	G	B

A	B	C#	D	E	F#	G#	A	B
①	2	3	4	5	6	7	8	9

The chord above, A C# E G B, is an A dominant ninth chord, and uses the symbol, A 9.

The distance from a note on an instrument, to that note again is called an octave, whether moving up or down.

The distance, when doubled, is called a double octave, or triple octave when the distance is tripled.

EXAMPLE:

(1)							(8)							(15)
G	A	B	C	D	E	F	G	A	B	C	D	E	F	G

From (1) to (8) is an octave; from (1) to (15) is two octaves (double octave), ascending.

From (15) to (8) is an octave; from (15) to (1) is two octaves (double octave), descending.

* = note is optional; can be left out

The next chord that we will examine in the extension chord family is the dominant eleventh, belonging to the dominant function group.

The formula for the dominant eleventh chord is 1 - 3 - 5 - ♭7 - 11, with the (11) actually being the (4), only up an octave.

EXAMPLE:

1	3	5	♭7	11
G	B	D	F	C

G	A	B	C	D	E	F♯	G	A	B	C
1	2	3	4	5	6	7	8	9	10	11

The chord above, G B D F C, is a G dominant eleventh chord and uses the symbol, G 11.

Notice that the distance between the (3) B and the (4) C is only a *semi-tone*, so always play the 11th up the octave, otherwise, expect an unpleasant sound.

Next in line is the dominant thirteenth chord, also belonging to the dominant function group.

The formula for the dominant thirteenth chord is 1 - 3 - 5 - ♭7 - 13, with the (13) actually being the (6) only up the octave, because of the close proximity to the(♭7).

EXAMPLE:

1	3	5	♭7								13
D	F♯	A	C								B

D	E	F♯	G	A	B	C♯	D	E	F♯	G	A	B
1	2	3	4	5	6	7	8	9	10	11	12	13

This chord, D F♯ A C B, is a dominant thirteenth, and uses the symbol, D 13.

Although the major sixth chord and the dominant thirteenth both share the (6) degree, they belong to different function groups.

This is because of the ♭7 being used in the dominant thirteenth chord.

Once the ♭7 is introduced into a chord it becomes part of the dominant group.

The (♭7) is usually added to a triad (3 note chord) already belonging to the dominant group, a chord built from the 5th or 7th degrees of a major scale, but theoretically a (♭7) can be added to any of the chords built from the degrees of a major scale, possibly changing the function of the chord.

Experiment with this just to see and hear some of the possibilities.

When playing dominant ninth, dominant eleventh, and dominant thirteenth chords, the fifth (5) is often omitted and the root note (1) or the (3) is doubled.

*When *adding extensions to a triad try not to change it's function within the key.*

EXAMPLE

Key of C major

CM7	Dm7	CM7	FM7 G7	CM7
/ / / /	/ / / /	/ / / /	/ / / /	/ / / /

The extension chords in the above example have the same function as they did as triad chords.

When extending a triad remember not to add a ♭7 to a tonic functioning chord, because adding a ♭7 to *any* triad makes that chord a member of the dominant chord family.

Remember that the major 7th chord should always be played in root position, in order to keep the major 7th and the root note from clashing, since they are only a semi - tone apart.

The only exception would be when the chord is being played spaced out over a wide range of the keyboard.

These are some rules that apply to extending chords, yet keeping them in the function to which they belong, in a particular key.

When extending a *Tonic* chord, try using only major 7th and major 6th additions.

This will help to center the sense of what key the music is in.

The further you get from the *Tonic sound,* the harder it will be to keep the music sounding like it belongs to a particular key.

When extending a *Dominant* chord, a ♭7 is always the first step.

There are *many* ways to extend a *Dominant* chord.

Since it is the chord that brings about the biggest change in a progression, there is lot's of room for experimentation, but always begin by adding a ♭7.

Adding a 6th to most triads other than a *Dominant* chord will not affect the function of that chord in a particular key.

Extension chords using C major as the starting point

M= Major   **m = minor**

Symbols	Formulas	Notes
C or C M	1,3,5	C E G
Cm	1,♭3,5	C E♭ G
Csus or Csus 4	1,4,5	C F G
C° or Cdim	1,♭3,♭5	C E♭ G♭
C+ or C aug	1,♯3, ♯5	C F G♯
C♭5 or C dim5	1,3,♭5	C E G♭
C6 or C M 6	1,3,5,6	C E G A
Cm6	1,♭3, 5,6	C E♭ G A
Cm6 / 9	1,♭3,5,6,9	C E♭ G A D
CM 7	1,3,5,7	C E G B
CM 9	1,3,5,7,9	C E G B D
CM 11	1,3,5,7,11	C E G B F
CM 13	1,3,5,7,13	C E G B A
Cm7	1,♭3,5,♭7	C E♭ G B♭
Cm7♭5	1,♭3,♭5,♭7	C E♭ G♭ B♭
Cm7♯5	1,♭3,♯5,♭7	C E♭ G♯ B♭
Cdim7	1,♭3,♭5,♭♭7	C E♭ G♭ B♭♭
C7	1,3,5,♭7	C E G B♭
C 9	1,3,5,♭7,9	C E G B♭ D
C11	1,3,5,♭7,9,11	C E G B♭ D F
C13	1,3,5,♭7,9,11,13	C E G B♭ D F A

Chapter 7

Melody and Rhythm

Music is comprised of three main components, melody, rhythm, and harmony.

Harmony is another word for chords, which means to *play* or *sing* more than one melody note simultaneously (at the same time).

Melody, often referred to as the tune of a song, means to play or sing one note at a time, usually in succession (one *after* the other).

Lyrics (words) are most often applied to the *melody* of a piece of music, although some music such as choir and choral music often uses *lyrics, in harmony, as the melody.*

In order to study melody properly, we will need to demonstrate on lines and spaces.

All of the information that you have studied in previous chapters will help you, greatly, in understanding music written on a staff (lines and spaces).

Rhythm is what gives music it's feel or syncopation (otherwise known as the beat).

Let's take a closer look at a staff (*lines and spaces*) and it's components.

62

These are some of the components of music written on a staff (lines and spaces).

First, let's begin with the lines and spaces themselves.

<u>5 Lines and 4 Spaces (between the lines)</u>

Now we will insert bar lines

← Bar line

Bar lines are used to mark the beginning and ending of bars, often called measures.

Bar lines work in conjunction with the time signature, which tells how many beats are in a measure and which note gets which count or value.

When the correct amount of note value has been completed, to satisfy the time signature, then a bar line is inserted.

If, for instance, the time signature is: $\frac{4}{4}$

EX:

$\underline{4}$ ← There are 4 beats in a measure

4 ← Quarter note (♩) counts as 1 beat

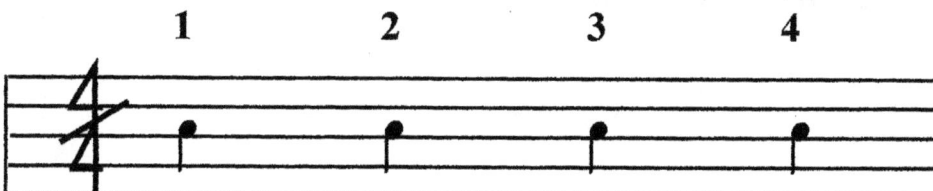

1　　2　　3　　4

There are two aspects to the music written on a staff; *melodic* and *rhythmic*.

The melody is found in the round part of a note, the part that sits on a line or in a space; while the rhythm is found in the stem, or lack of a stem, in the case of a whole note.

EXAMPLE:

← rhythm (feel)

melody (sound) →

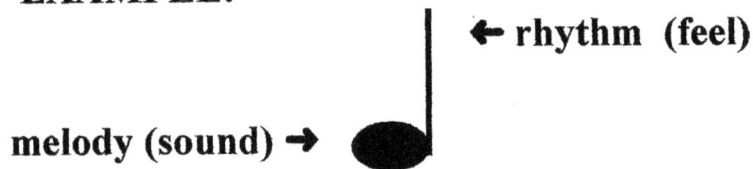

The melody (or melodic) part of a note tells the sound (or pitch) that the note will have; while the stem (or rhythmic) part of a note tells the duration (how long the note is to be held) and determines how the music will feel.

Melody notes can also be very helpful when trying to find out what key a piece of music is written in (which we will examine later in chapter 11).

The names of the lines and spaces depend on which *clef* is placed in the signature bar.

There are several clefs used in music, enabling us to read or write music for many different instruments, and also for voice.

Since we are studying music for piano, the only clefs that we will be using are the treble and bass clefs.

However, there are instruments besides the piano which use music written upon the bass and treble clefs.

Clefs

Treble Clef   Bass Clef

These clefs (symbols), when inserted at the beginning of the lead-off bar, establishes what the names of the lines and spaces will be, throughout the piece of music.

When the *treble clef* is placed in the lead-off bar, the lines (starting with the bottom line) are E, G, B, D, F and the spaces are F, A, C, E.

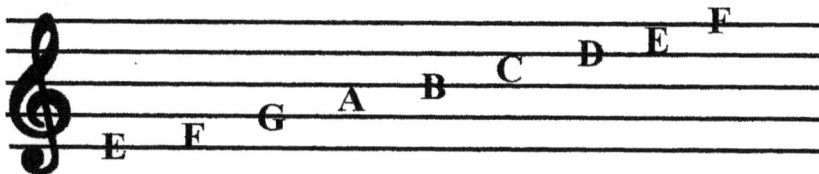

Ways to remember lines and spaces in the treble clef:

Lines: Every Good Boy Does Fine - E G B D F
Spaces: F A C E

The middle curl of the treble clef fixes itself around the second line of the staff, establishing it as the G line.

For this reason, the treble clef is also sometimes referred to as the G clef.

When the bass clef is placed at the lead-off bar, the lines (starting from the bottom line) are G, B, D, F, A and the spaces are A, C, E, G.

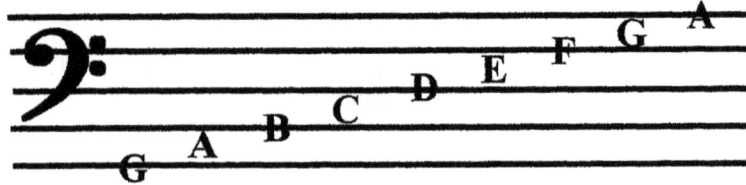

Ways to remember lines and spaces in the bass clef:

Lines: Good Boys Do Fine Always - G B D F A
Spaces: All Cows Eat Grass - A C E G

The bass clef curls around the F line; for this reason, it is sometimes referred to as the F clef.

The treble clef and the bass clef are often joined together by a long bar line that extends from the F line of the treble clef to the G line of the bass clef.

This is called a stave and is written in this way to join music played on the upper and lower ends of an instrument, usually a piano.

The treble clef contains all of the music played above middle C, which is the C note found closest to the middle of a piano or keyboard.

The bass clef contains all of the music played below middle C.

As far as lines and spaces are concerned, when middle C is written, it is written on a leger line, *the lines found above, below, or between the treble clef and the bass clef of a staff.*

The A and B notes above the treble clef are both written on leger lines.

The middle C between the treble clef and the bass clef is also written on a leger line.

As previously stated, the rhythm is what gives the music it's feel.

By reading notes on the lines and spaces, we know what notes (or sounds) to play on an instrument, but without the stem we would not know how the music is to be spaced or *syncopated*.

A whole note is the only note which has no stem and lasts for the duration of a 4/4 bar of music.

All other notes have stems, *only the whole note has no stem.*

The following example contains the *rhythmic values* of the notes in music, up to the sixteenth note.

EXAMPLE:

	𝅝	𝅗𝅥	𝅘𝅥	𝅘𝅥𝅮	𝅘𝅥𝅯
BEATS:	4	2	1	½	¼
NOTES:	whole note	half note	quarter note	eighth note	sixteenth note

Rhythmic value = how long a note is to be held from start to finish.
A dot (.) coming after a note counts as ½ of that note.

The three main components that enable you to read and understand the music written on a staff are:

The Clef:

Treble

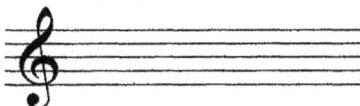

or

Bass

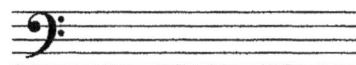

The Time Signature:

EX.1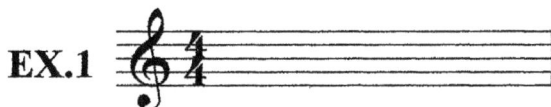

EX.2

EX.3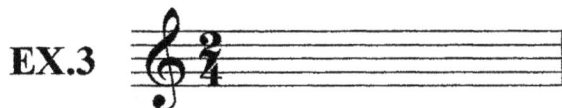

The Key Signature:

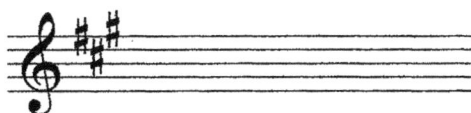

69

*The clef: Determines what the lines and spaces will be called.

You can see why the *clef* is a must-have for identifying the notes on lines and spaces.

*The time signature: Dictates how many *(top number)* of what note values (*bottom number*) each bar must contain.

If the note values were evenly and properly distributed, from one bar to the next, you could figure out the *time signature*; but it is much easier having it indicated at the beginning of a piece of music.

*The key signature: Identifies what scale (key) the music is to be played in and tells which notes, if any, are to be altered (with #'s or ♭'s) in order to keep the tones and semi-tones properly spaced within the scale.
This is the reason for using #'s and ♭'s; to keep the tones and semi-tones properly spaced.

Unless you want to always play in the key of C Major (no #'s or ♭'s), then a *key signature* also is very necessary.

Chapter 8

<u>Time Signature, Notes & Rests</u>

      In bars 1 through 5 below, each individual bar, although different in appearence because of the notes, have the same time duration value; meaning that each individual bar takes up the same amount of time from start to finish.

      However, this does not mean that they sound alike, even though they are all F notes.

      The thing that gives each bar it's own sound is the fact that they're written in different rhythmic patterns.

      The reason that they all fit into the 4/4 time signature is because, mathematically, each bar contains the equivalent of 4 quarter (♩) notes.

whole note   half notes   quarter notes   eighth notes

sixteenth notes

In order to get a better understanding, let's examine each bar individually, starting with bar 1.

1

The whole note in bar 1 is struck on the one, of a one - two - three - four count, and held down (sounded) for the entire count.

Strike the note on the count of one and hold it down (do not release it) while counting one -two - three -four in your head.

At the end of the four count, just before the one count of the next bar, release the note.

Let's take a look at bar 2, containing two half notes.

A half note is just what the name implies, 1/2 of a whole note.

Since a whole note occupies a four note count and since a half note is 1/2 of a whole note, it gets a two count and two half notes add up to a whole note, completing a bar of 4/4.

2

2

Although a half note gets a 1-2 count, it is only pressed on the one and held down until the two count is finished.

Since, a bar of 4/4 contains two half notes, for the first note we press down on the one count, continue to hold for the two count, release, press down again on the three count, continue to hold for the four count, and release just before what would be the one count of the next bar.

EXAMPLE:

Count >   1 - 2 - 3 - 4
              press   hold press hold

3

In a bar of 4/4 there are four quarter notes; with each note receiving a one count.

In other words, while *counting 1 -2 -3 -4*, you are *playing 1-2-3-4* .

Here we see the true 4/4 time signature being executed, four beats (or counts) to a bar, with each quarter note getting a count.

The reason that one whole note can take the place of four quarter notes is because one whole note is the equivalent of (or contains) four quarter notes.

EXAMPLE:

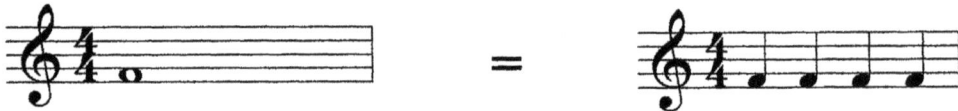

This is why a bar of one whole note can use the 4/4 signature, because one whole note does indeed contain four quarter notes.

4

Bar 4 contains eight eighth notes and has a 4/4 time signature.

Once again, the reason that a 4/4 time signature is used, is because the eight eighth notes are equivalent to one whole note, *or* two half notes, *or* four quarter notes.

Since *every quarter note contains two eighth notes,* instead of counting 1 -2 -3 -4, a bar of eight eighth notes would be counted as **1-&-2-&-3-&-4-&.**

The 1 -2 -3 -4 would still come at the same spot where quarter notes would be played, but the difference is, you now have twice as many notes to be played in the same amount of space and time.

This means that, as you count 1-2-3-4, there is now an extra note that comes after each number, without changing the speed at which you are counting and playing.

EXAMPLE:

count   1   2   3   4

count   1   &   2   &   3   &   4   &

When counting eighth notes, whether silently or out loud, count 1 and 2 and 3 and etc.
This is what the & stands for (and).

5

1   2   3   4

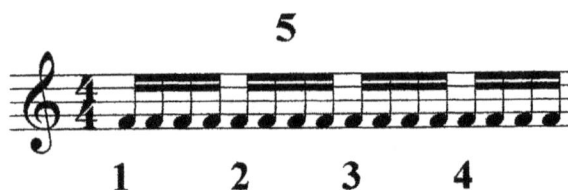

Bar **5** contains sixteen sixteenth notes and has a 4/4 time signature.

Sixteen sixteenth notes are equivalent to one whole note, *or* two half notes, *or* four quarter notes, *or* eight eighth notes.

Since *one quarter note contains four sixteenth notes,* instead of counting 1-2-3-4, a 4/4 bar of sixteenth notes would be counted as 1-*e*-&-*a*-2-*e*-&-*a*-3-*e*-&-*a*-4-*e*-&-*a*.

The 1-2-3-4 would still come at the same spot where the quarter notes would be played, but the difference is, you now have four times as many notes to be played in the same amount of space and time.

This means that, as you play 1-2-3-4, there is now three *extra* notes that come after each number, without changing the points where the 1-2-3-4 fall.

EXAMPLE:

count   1   2   3   4

count   1 *e* & *a* 2 *e* & *a* 3 *e* & *a* 4 *e* & *a*

The *e* and *a* are not meant as the names for the notes, they are used to mark where the beats fall.

They are pronounced one -*e* - and - *a*, (e, being the long sound of the vowel, e; a being the short sound of the vowel, a)

In the following examples, we will use the rests in combination with the notes that have the same time value.

Because a whole note and a whole rest each fill a whole bar, we will follow a whole note bar with a whole rest bar.

We will stop at the sixteenth note and the sixteenth rest because the remaining notes and rests are not applicable to the music that we will be touching on, for the simple fact that they are so quickly executed.

However, if and when you reach that level of playing and music-reading skill, you will have already become equipped with the knowledge of them, through advanced study.

EXAMPLE 1

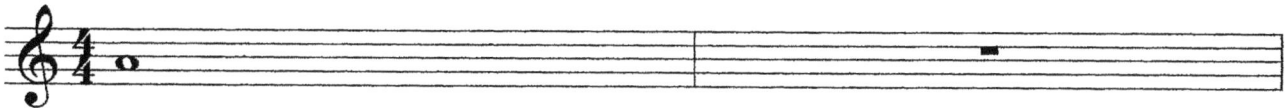

EXAMPLE 2

EXAMPLE 3

EXAMPLE 4

Let's examine each example more closely, starting with example # 1.

EXAMPLE 1

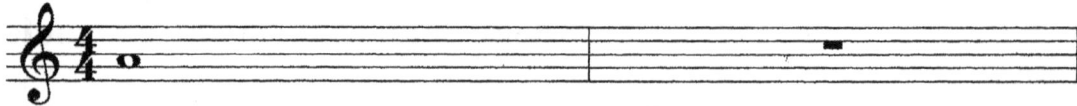

count	1	2	3	4	1	2	3	4
	P	H	H	H	R	R	R	R

P = play   H = hold   R = rest

In example 1, the whole note is played on the one count and held down throughout the two, three, and four counts.

The whole rest, in the second bar, is counted (but not played) for a one, two, three, four count.

EXAMPLE 2

count	1	2	3	4	1	2	3	4
	P	H	R	R	P	R	P	R

In example 2, the half note in the first bar is played on the one count and held down for the two count.

The half rest in the first bar is counted, as two silent beats, on the three and four counts.

The two quarter notes in the second bar are played on the one and three counts.

The two quarter rests in the second bar are counted, as silent beats, on the two and four counts.

EXAMPLE 3

count	1	&	2	&	3	&	4	&
	P	R	P	R	P	R	P	R

In example 3, on the first half of the one count, an eighth note is played.

On the second half of the one count (*the & half*) an eighth rest is counted.

It is the same process on the remaining second, third, and fourth counts; on the first half of the count an eighth note is played and an eighth rest is counted on the second half of the count.

Notice, while playing this bar, that it sounds very similiar to a 4/4 bar of quarter notes.

This is because there is a note being played on each of the one, two, three, and four counts.

The difference between example 3 and a 4/4 bar of quarter notes is that the notes in example 3 should sound slightly shorter in duration, because in example 3 the notes are eighth notes.

EXAMPLE 4

count   1 *e & a* 2 *e & a* 3 *e & a* 4 *e & a*

    P R P   R   P R P   R   P R P   R   P R P   R

       Once you begin to play example 4, you will probably notice the similarities between this example and a 4/4 bar of straight eighth notes.

       The only difference is that the sixteenth notes in example 4 will sound for a slightly shorter time, but they will each have the 1 & 2 & 3 & 4 & feel to them.

EXAMPLE 4

count   1 *e & a* 2 *e & a* 3 *e & a* 4 *e & a*

    P R P R   P R P R   P R P R   P R P R

count   1   &   2   &   3   &   4   &

       When a, **C**, is in the time signature, as in the above example, it means the same as 4/4 in the time signature.

       It is an abbreviation for the 4/4 time signature.

Remember that in time signatures: The top note tells how many of the bottom number (type of note; or the equivalent) are to be played in one bar.

We have already familiarized ourselves with the 4/4 time signature, so now it's time to proceed further.

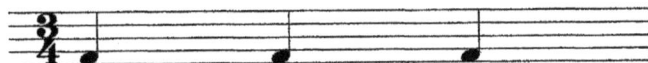

3 *quarter* notes to 1 bar

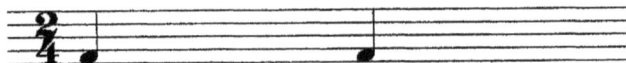

2 *quarter* notes to a bar

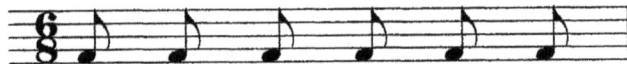

6 *eighth* notes to a bar

12 *eighth* notes to a bar

Although, there are other time signatures, for all practical purposes we will confine our studies to the above time signatures, along with the 4/4 time signature.

82

Bar 1 displays exactly what the time
signature calls for; 3 quarter notes (♩) to one bar.

Bar 2 contains 3 quarter rests (𝄽) which is
the equivalent, in silence, to 3 quarter notes.

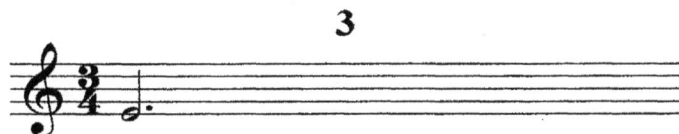

Bar 3 contains 1 dotted half note (♩.). 1
half note equals 2 quarter notes (♩) and a
dot (.) counts for 1/2 of whatever note it
comes after, in this case, a half note (♩), so
the value of the (.) is 1 quarter note.
2+1 = 3

Bar 4 contains 6 eighth notes (♪) and
since 1 quarter note (♩) equals 2 eighth
notes ; 6 eighth notes equal 3 quarter notes .

1

In example 1, the bar contains 2 quarter notes, which is exactly what the time signature calls for.

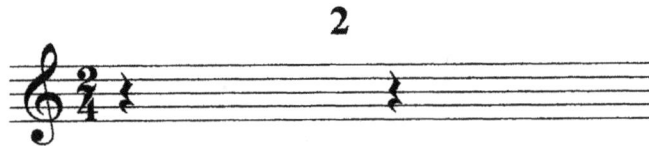

2

Example 2 contains the equivalent of 2 quarter notes by using 2 quarter rests.

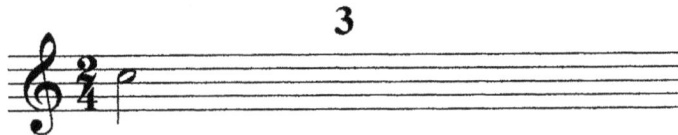

3

Example 3 contains 1 half note, which in itself, equals 2 quarter notes.

4

Example 4 contains 1 eighth note, followed by 2 eighth rests, ending with another eighth note.

Together, they are the equivalent of 4 eighth notes or 2 quarter notes, fulfilling the 2/4 time signature.

84

This bar contains the exact equivalent of what the key signature calls for, 6 eighth notes.

Bar 2 contains an eighth rest, followed by two eighth notes, another eighth rest, ending with a quarter note.

If you add them up, you will find that they complete a bar of 6/8.

Bar 3 contains 3 quarter rests and since each quarter rest contains 2 eighth rests, the 3 quarter rests complete the bar.

In bar 4; 2 eighth notes, 1 quarter note, (containing 2 eighth notes), and 2 more eighth notes equal 1 bar of 6/8.

Bars 1 and 2 have the exact same note value, although the stems are joined together in bar 1, for the sake of making the notes look less scattered.

Each of these bars contain the exact equivalent of what the key signature calls for, 6 eighth notes.

In writing notes and rests on a staff, the idea is to do it as neatly and as uniform as possible, also using as few notes or rests as possible.

This makes the music easier to read and understand.

For example:

Although the 4 quarter rests have the same rest value as the 1 whole rest, it makes more sense to write it as the one whole rest, for the simple fact that, once the reader sees the one whole rest, the point is taken immediately.

Also there is less clutter.

Bar 1 contains 12 eighth notes, just as the time signature dictates.

Bar 2 contains 6 quarter notes, which can be divided into 12 eighth notes, thereby fulfilling the 12/8 time signature.

This bar contains 6 eighth rests and 6 eighth notes, completing a bar of 12/8 time.

Chapter 9

<u>Understanding Key Signatures</u>

Included, between the clef and the time signature, in the first bar of a piece of music, is the key signature.

Example 1:

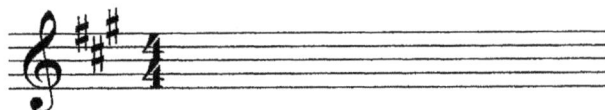

The purpose of the key signature is to alert the reader to all of the notes in the piece that will be affected by (♯'s or ♭'s).

For instance, in the key signature above, every F, C, and G note will be sharp.

When a note is affected by a key signature (sharp or flat), that note is affected throughout the entire piece of music.

The only time that a note can be changed from what it is in the key signature is when a natural (♮) is inserted to remove the sharp or flat, restoring the note to it's natural state.

A natural, however, is only good for the particular bar in which it appears, after that bar, the affected note returns to whatever it is in the key signature.

Sharps, flats, or naturals written into a piece of music, but not included in the key signature are called accidentals.

Example :

In bars 1, 2, and 3, the notes are to be played according to what they are in the key signature (sharp).

In bar 4, the first two G notes are sharp, according to the key signature, but the third G note has a natural in front of it, which cancels out the sharp in the key signature.

However, in bar 5 the sharp in the key signature has been restored, because the natural only applies from it's insertion until the end of *that particular* bar.

There is a definite order to the way the sharps and flats are written in a key signature.

The order of sharps:

F♯, C♯, G♯, D♯, A♯, E♯, B♯

In other words:

A. In a key signature with *one* sharp, the sharp will appear on the F line.

B. In a key signature with *two* sharps, the sharps will appear on the F line and C space.

C. In a key signature with *three* sharps, the sharps will appear on the F, C, and G line and spaces.

D. In a key signature with *four* sharps, the sharps will appear on the F, C, G, and D lines and spaces.

E. In a key signature with *five* sharps, the sharps will appear on the F, C, G, D, and A lines and spaces.

F. In a key signature with *six* sharps, the sharps will appear on the F, C, G, D, A, and E lines and spaces.

G. In a key signature with *seven* sharps, the sharps will appear on the F, C, G, D, A, E, and B lines and spaces.

*Keep in mind that E♯, is really F, and B♯, is really C.

Sharp Key Signatures In Major

C Major

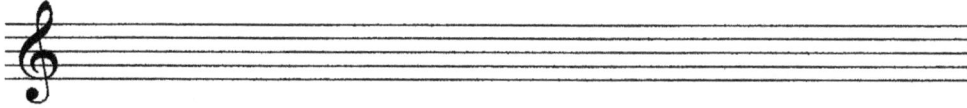

G Major

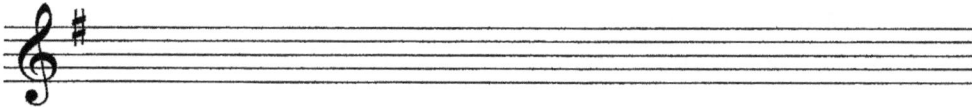

D Major

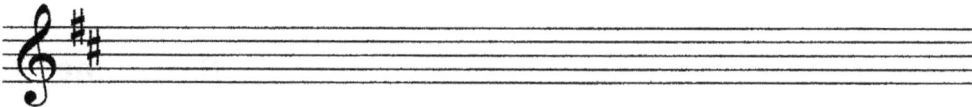

A Major

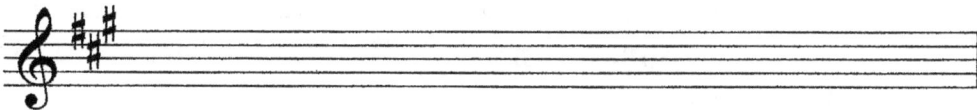

E Major

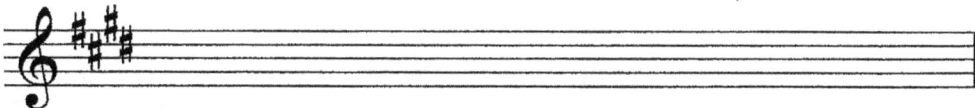

B Major

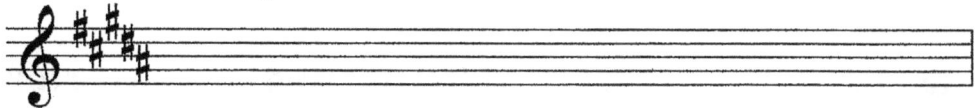

F# Major

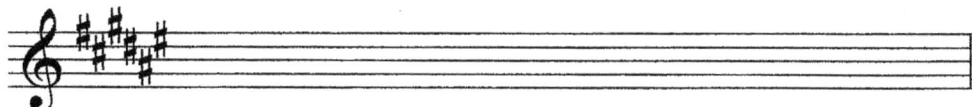

C# Major

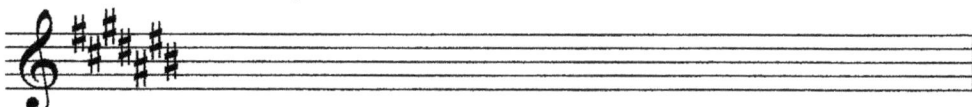

* Remember that C Major has no sharps or flats

The order of flats :

Bb, Eb, Ab, Db, Gb, Cb, Fb

In other words:

A. In a key signature with *one* flat, the flat
   would appear on the B line.
B. In a key signature with *two* flats, the flats
   would appear on the B line and E space.
C. In a key signature with *three* flats, the flats
   would appear on the B, E, and A line
   and spaces.
D. In a key signature with *four* flats, the flats
   would appear on the B, E, A, and D
   lines and spaces.
E. In a key signature with *five* flats, the flats
   would appear on the B, E, A, D, and G
   lines and spaces.
F. In a key signature with *six* flats, the flats
   would appear on the B, E, A, D, G, and C
   lines and spaces.
G. In a key signature with *seven* flats, the flats
   would appear on the B, E, A, D, G, C,
   and F lines and spaces.

*Keep in mind that Cb, is really B, and Fb, is really E.

Flat Key Signatures In Major

C Major

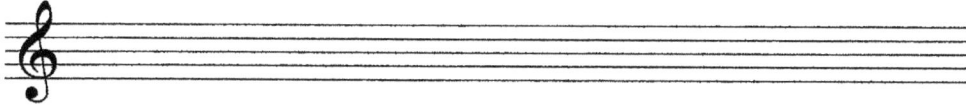

F Major

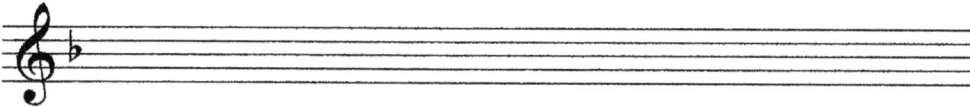

B♭ Major

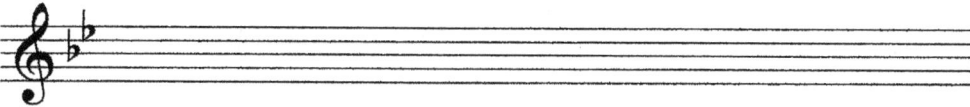

E♭ Major

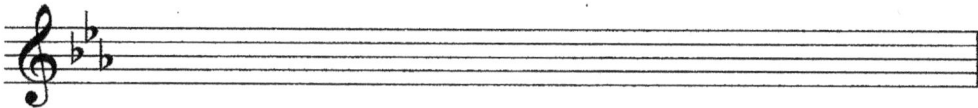

A♭ Major

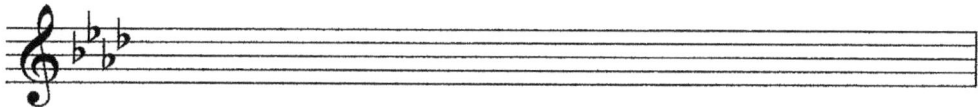

D♭ Major

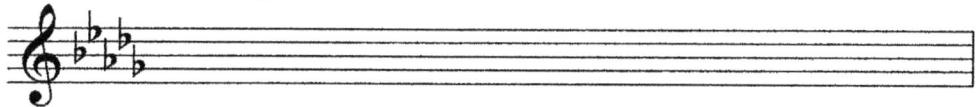

G♭ Major

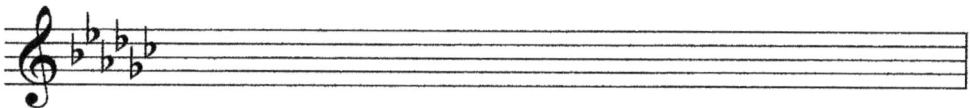

C♭ Major

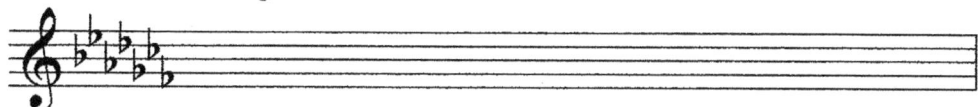

* **Remember that C Major has no sharps or flats**

Chapter 10

<u>Major Scales & Their Chords</u>

Because playing the right melody notes with the right chords is so crucial to sounding good, we have included, in this chapter, all of the major scales with their chords.

Along with each chord, we have inserted the notes that are acceptable and also the notes that are unacceptable for each chord.

Once you become familiar with these chords and learn which notes *not* to play, along with each particular chord, soloing becomes easier.

Try practicing the chords, one at a time, while soloing (playing melody notes).

Major Scales and Their Chords

C Major Scale

1	2	3	4	5	6	7	8
C	D	E	F	G	A	B	C

Chords In C Major	Play	Don't Play
1 = C E G = C	C,D,E,G,A,	F,B
2 = D F A = Dm	D,F,G,A,B,C	E
3 = E G B = Em	E,G,A,B,D	F,C
4 = F A C = F	F,G,A,C, D	E,B
5 = G B D = G	G.A.B,D,E,F	C
6 = A C E = Am	A,C,D,E,G	B,F
7 = B D F = B dim	B,D,F,G,A	C,E

G Major Scale

1	2	3	4	5	6	7	8
G	A	B	C	D	E	F#	G

Chords In G Major	Play	Don't Play
1 = G B D = G	G,A,B,D,E	F#, C#
2 = A C E = Am	G,A,C,D,E,F#	B
3 = B D F# = Bm	B,D,E,F#,A	C,G
4 = C E G = C	C,D,E,G,A	B,F#
5 = D F# A = D	D,E,F#,A,B,C	G
6 = E G B = Em	E,G,A,B,D	F#,C
7 = F# A C = F#dim	F#,A,C,D,E	G,B

D Major Scale

1	2	3	4	5	6	7	8
D	E	F♯	G	A	B	C♯	D

Chords In D Major	Play	Don't Play
1 = D F♯ A = D	D,E,F♯,A,B	G,C♯
2 = E G B = Em	E,G,A,B,C♯,D	F♯
3 = F♯ A C♯ = F♯m	F♯,A,B,C♯,E	G,D
4 = G B D = G	G,A,B,D,E	C♯,F♯
5 = A C♯ E = A	A,B,C♯,E,F♯,G	D
6 = B D F♯ = Bm	B,D,E,F♯,A	C♯,G
7 = C♯ E G = C♯dim	C♯,E,G,A,B	D,F♯

A Major Scale

1	2	3	4	5	6	7	8
A	B	C#	D	E	F#	G#	A

Chords In A Major	Play	Don't Play
1 = A C# E = A	A,B,C#,E,F#	D,G#
2 = B D F# = Bm	B,D,E,F#,G#,A	C#
3 = C# E G# = C#m	C#,E,F#,G#,B	D,A
4 = D F# A = D	D,E,F#,A,B	G#,C#
5 = E G# B = E	E,F#,G#,B,C#,D	A
6 = F# A C# = F#m	F#,A,B,C#,E	G,D
7 = G# B D = G# dim	G#,B,D,E,F#	C#,A

E Major Scale

1	2	3	4	5	6	7	8
E	F#	G#	A	B	C#	D#	E

Chords In A Major	Play	Don't Play
1 = E G# B = E	E,F#,G#,B,C#	A,D#
2 = F# A C# = F#m	F#,A,B,C#,D#,E	G
3 = G# B D# = G#m	G#,B,C#,D#,F#	A,E
4 = A C# E = A	A,B,C#,E,F#	G#,D
5 = B D# F# = B	B,C#,D#,F#,G#,A	E
6 = C# E G# = C#m	C#,E,F#,G#,B	D#,A
7 = D# F# A = D#dim	D#,F#,A,B,C#	E,G#

B Major Scale

1	2	3	4	5	6	7	8
B	C#	D#	E	F#	G#	A#	B

Chords In B Major	Play	Don't Play
1 = B D# F# = B	B,C#,D#,F#,G#,	E,A
2 = C# E G# = C#m	C#,E,F#,G#,B,A#	D
3 = D# F# A# = D#m	D#,F#,G#,A#C#	E,B
4 = E G# B = E	E,F#,G#,B,C#	D#,A
5 = F# A# C# = F#	F#,G#,A#,C#,D#,E	B
6 = G# B D# = G#m	G#,B,C#,D#,F#	A#,E
7 = A# C# E = A# dim	A#,C#,E,F#G#	B,D#

100

F♯ Major Scale

1	2	3	4	5	6	7	8
F♯	G♯	A♯	B	C♯	D♯	E♯	F♯

Chords In F♯ Major	Play	Don't Play
1 = F♯ A♯ C♯ = F♯	F♯,G♯,A♯,C♯,D♯,	B,E♯
2 = G♯ B D♯ = G♯m	F♯,G♯,B,C♯,D♯,E♯	A♯
3 = A♯ C♯ E♯ = A♯m	A♯,C♯,D♯,E♯,G♯	B,F♯
4 = B D♯ F♯ = B	B,C♯,D♯,F♯,G♯	E♯,A♯
5 = C♯ E♯ G♯ = C♯	C♯,D♯,E♯,G♯,A♯,B	F♯
6 = D♯ F♯ A♯ = D♯m	D♯,F♯,G♯,A♯,C♯	E♯,B
7 = E♯ G♯ B = E♯dim	E♯,G♯,B,C♯,D♯	F♯,A♯

C♯ Major Scale

1	2	3	4	5	6	7	8
C♯	D♯	E♯	F♯	G♯	A♯	B♯	C♯

Chords In C♯ Major	Play	Don't Play
1 = C♯ E♯ G♯ = C♯	C♯,D♯,E♯,G♯,A♯	F♯,B♯
2 = D♯ F♯ A♯ = D♯m	D♯,F♯,G♯,A♯,B♯,C♯	E♯
3 = E♯ G♯ B♯ = E♯m	E♯,G♯,A♯,B♯,D♯	F♯,C♯
4 = F♯ A♯ C♯ = F♯	F♯,G♯,A♯,C♯,D♯	B♯,E♯
5 = G♯ B♯ D♯ = G♯	G♯,A♯,B♯,D♯,E♯,F♯	C♯
6 = A♯ C♯ E♯ = A♯m	A♯,C♯,D♯,E♯,G♯	B♯,F♯
7 = B♯ D♯ F♯ = B dim	B♯,D♯,F♯,G♯,A♯	C♯,E♯

*   *Remember that in order to move up, by one tone, from E♯, the F needs to be made double sharp (F♯♯), actually becoming G.*
    The same theory applies when moving up, by one tone, from B♯, the C needs to be made double sharp (C♯♯), actually becoming D.

102

F Major scale

1	2	3	4	5	6	7	8
F	G	A	B♭	C	D	E	F

Chords in F Major	Play	Don't Play
1 = F A C = F	F,G,A,C,D	B♭,E
2 = G B♭ D = Gm	G,B♭,C,D,E,F	A
3 = A C E = Am	A,C,D,E,G	B♭,F
4 = B♭ D F = B♭	B♭,C,D,F,G,	E,A
5 = C E G = C	C,D,E,G,A,B♭	F
6 = D F A = Dm	D,F,G,A,C	E,B♭
7 = E G B♭ = E dim	E,G,B♭,C,D	F,A

103

Bb Major scale

1	2	3	4	5	6	7	8
Bb	C	D	Eb	F	G	A	Bb

Chords in Bb Major	Play	Don't Play
1 = Bb D F = Bb	Bb,C,D,F,G	A,E
2 = C Eb G = Cm	C,Eb,F,G,A,Bb	D
3 = D F A = Dm	D,F,G,A,C	Eb,Bb
4 = Eb G Bb = Eb	Eb,F,G,Bb,C	A,D
5 = F A C = F	F,G,A,C,D,Eb	Bb
6 = G Bb D = Gm	G,Bb,C,D,F	A,Eb
7 = A C Eb = A dim	A,C,Eb,F,G	Bb,D

104

E♭ Major scale

1	2	3	4	5	6	7	8
E♭	F	G	A♭	B♭	C	D	E♭

Chords in E♭ Major	Play	Don't Play
1 = E♭ G B♭ = E♭	E♭,F,G,B♭,C,	A♭,D
2 = F A♭ C = Fm	F,A♭,B♭,C,D,E♭	G
3 = G B♭ D = Gm	G,B♭,C,D,F	A♭.E♭
4 = A♭ C E♭ = A♭	A♭,B♭,C,E♭,F	D,G
5 = B♭ D F = B♭	B♭,C,D,F,G,A♭	E♭
6 = C E♭ G = Cm	C,E♭,F,G,B♭	D,A♭
7 = D F A♭ =D dim	D,F,A♭,B♭,C	E♭,G

105

Ab Major   scale

1	2	3	4	5	6	7	8
Ab	Bb	C	Db	Eb	F	G	Ab

Chords in Ab Major	Play	Don't Play
1 = Ab C Eb = Ab	Ab,Bb,C,Eb,F	Db,G
2 = Bb Db F = Bbm	Bb,Db,Eb,F,G,Ab	C
3 = C Eb G = Cm	C,Eb,F,G,Bb	Db,Ab
4 = Db F Ab = Db	Db,Eb,F,Ab,Bb	C,G
5 = Eb G Bb= Eb	Eb,F,G,Bb,C,Db	Ab
6 = F Ab C = Fm	F,Ab,Bb,C,Eb	G,Db
7 = G Bb Db= G dim	G,Bb,Db,E,b,F	Ab,C

D♭ Major scale

1	2	3	4	5	6	7	8
D♭	E♭	F	G♭	A♭	B♭	C	D♭

Chords in D♭ Major	Play	Don't Play
1 = D♭ F A♭ = D♭	D♭,E♭F,A♭,B♭	G,C
2 = E♭ G♭ B♭ = E♭m	E♭,G♭,A♭,B♭,C,D♭	F
3 = F A♭ C = Fm	F,A♭,B♭,C,E♭	G♭,D♭
4 = G♭ B♭ D♭ = G♭	G♭,A♭,B♭,D♭,E♭	C,F
5 = A♭ C E♭ = A♭	A♭,B♭,C,E♭,F♭,G♭	D♭
6 = B♭ D♭ F = B♭m	B♭,D♭,E♭,F,A♭	C,G♭
7 = C E♭ G♭= C dim	C,E♭,G♭,A♭,B♭	D♭,F

G♭ Major scale

1	2	3	4	5	6	7	8
G♭	A♭	B♭	C♭	D♭	E♭	F	G♭

Chords in G♭ Major	Play	Don't Play
1 = G♭ B♭ D♭ = G♭	G♭,A♭,B♭,D♭,E♭,	C♭,F
2 = A♭ C♭ E♭ = A♭m	A♭,C♭,D♭,E♭,F,G♭	B♭
3 = B♭ D♭ F = B♭m	B♭,D♭,E♭,F,A♭	C♭,G♭
4 = C♭ E♭ G♭ = C♭	C♭,D♭,E♭,A♭,G♭	F,B♭
5 = D♭ F A♭ = D♭	D♭,E♭,F,A♭,B♭,C♭	G♭
6 = E♭ G♭ B♭ = E♭m	E♭,G♭,A♭,B♭,D♭	F,C♭
7 = F A♭ C♭ = F dim	F,A♭,B♭,D♭,E♭	G♭,C♭

108

C♭ Major scale

1	2	3	4	5	6	7	8
C♭	D♭	E♭	F♭	G♭	A♭	B♭	C♭

Chords in C♭ Major	Play	Don't Play
1 = C♭ E♭ G♭= C♭	C♭,D♭,E♭,G♭,A♭	F,B♭
2 = D♭ F♭ A♭= D♭m	D♭,F♭,G♭,A♭,B♭,C♭	E♭
3 = E♭ G♭ B♭= E♭m	E♭,G♭,A♭,B♭,D♭	F♭,C♭
4 = F♭ A♭ C♭ = F♭	F♭,G♭,A♭,C♭,D♭	E♭,B♭
5 = G♭ B♭ D♭ = G♭	G♭,A♭,B♭,D♭,E♭,F♭	C♭
6 = A♭ C♭ E♭= A♭m	A♭,C♭,D♭,E♭,G♭	B♭,F♭
7 = B♭ D♭ F♭= B♭ dim	B♭,D♭,F♭,G♭,A♭	C♭,E♭

Chapter 11

<u>Melody, Rhythm, & Harmony Combined</u>

This is the section where we bring all of the components together.

To begin, we must know how to construct a major scale, separating the notes by the proper tones and semi-tones.

Knowing this, we can write out the C major scale, using a 4/4 time signature.

Because there are no sharps or flats required in the scale of C major, the key signature is left blank.

<u>C major scale : C D E F G A B C</u>

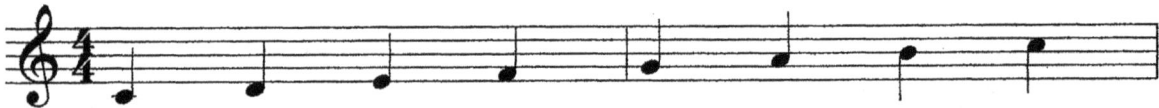

Using the (ta - ski - ta - ski - ta) method, form the seven triads taken from the C major scale.

C   Dm   Em   F   G   Am   B dim   C

The (**C**) time signature above is an abbreviation for the 4/4 time signature found in the previous example; it means exactly the same thing.

It is now time to group the chords according to their functions in the key of C major.

Tonic	Sub - dominant	Dominant
C Em Am	Dm F	G B(dim)

Next, let us establish the chord pattern which we will use.

Since we are in the key of C major, let's begin with a chord from the *Tonic* function group.

In order to give the music a definite sense of the key of C major, there is no better chord to begin with, than a C chord.

C
/ / / /

Keeping things simple, we can add a Dm chord.

C Dm
/ / / / / / / /

At this point, we are concerned with the chord progression only.

After this is established, we will focus on combining melody with the chords.

Moving in the natural progression of the chords in C major let's complete this chord progression.

C Dm Em F G C
/ / / / / / / / / / / / / / / / / / / /

For now, we will be using chords in their root positions, in order to keep the flow as connected as possible.

So that you will be able to read chords on lines and spaces, as well as chords in short hand, as they appear on the previous page, we will move back and forth between them.

For obvious reasons, when melody is included, we will be using only lines and spaces (staffs).

The progression below is the same as the one on the previous page.

The chords are meant to be played with the left hand, while the melody is played with the right hand.

Using the tips in the *Major Scales and Their Chords* section, let's play some melody along with the chord progression.

L= Left Hand   R= Right Hand

An important thing to remember, when combining chords and melody is that in a *melody*, a note can follow or come before a note that is only a semi-tone away from that note.

EXAMPLE : 1

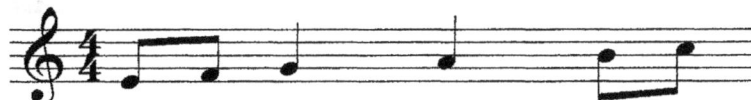

In this melody, E goes directly to F and B goes directly to C.

However, if you were to play a C major chord along with this melody, the C in the chord would clash with the B in the melody and the E in the chord would clash with the F in the melody.

EXAMPLE : 2

Although the F note comes on the & of 1, it will still clash with the E note in the chord because the chord is sustained until the 2 count begins.

On the 4 beat, there is a direct clash between the B note in the melody and the C note in the chord, but, because the B note is played so far away from the C note, it could be used as a C M7.

Note that on the 3 beat the A note, in the melody, along with the C,E,G notes in the chord, form a C M6 chord.

C E G A

Seeing that the two pairs of notes (B,C) and (E,F) clash, when played at the same time, tells us that while playing a C major chord we should avoid playing a B or F note in the melody.

If you can't play these two notes (B or F) with the C major chord, what other notes could we substitute for them?

The answer is ; any other notes found in the scale of C major.

A, C, D, E, G

By the same principle, after moving to the next chord in the C major family, which is Dm, the F and the B notes are permitted in the melody, but you wouldn't play an E note, in the melody, because it would clash with the F note in the Dm chord.

EXAMPLE

The G in the melody, along with the D,F,A in the Dm chord, forms a Dm (add11) chord.

D,F,G,A

Also, the B in the melody, along with the D,F,A notes in the Dm chord, forms a Dm6 chord.

D,F,A,B

A major 7 (the natural seveth degree in a major scale) can, theoretically, be played along with any chord, not belonging to the *dominant function*, as long as the 7 is not played in close proximity to the 1 (root note).

Let's explore this melody, written in the 3/4 time signature.

3/4 time signature is often referred to as waltz time, because it is the time signature that most waltzes are written in.

A key signature has been purposely omitted.

In bars 7, 8, and 16, we have introduced a *dotted half note.*

When a dot (.) comes after a note, the dot counts as half of whatever the value of the note is.

The dot coming after a half note has the value of one quarter note, a quarter note being one half of the two quarter notes contained in a half note.

Keeping this in mind, let's begin to work our way through bars 1 through 16.

First of all, in order to understand the feel of 3/4 time, imagine people dancing to waltz music, doing the 1-2-3 step.

play >> P P P P R P P P R P P P

Learning to put your fingers into position, before actually playing, can help you to instinctively come down on the notes to be played, while counting both, the notes and rests, in your head.

The only way to know where to position your fingers beforehand is to look over the music prior to playing it, seeing the complete span of the music, from the lowest note to the highest note.

＊ Note : In a bar of 3/4 you will not find a whole note or a whole rest, because the time signature itself states that there are only three quarter notes in a bar and there are four quarter notes in a whole note.

In bars **5** through **8**, all of the notes are to be played; there are no rests.

Although the time signature is 3/4, the eighth notes, in bars 5 and 6, are still counted as 1 &, 2 &, 3 & ; but the waltz feel makes them occur more quickly.

In other words, a bar of eighth notes in 4/4 time will sound different from a bar of eighth notes in 3/4 time.

Because the majority of popular songs are written in 4/4 time and due to our familiarity with the 4/4 feel, a bar of 3/4 could feel incomplete, because of the missing 4 count.

And, because of going from the 3 count right back to the 1 count, in 3/4, everything has to happen more quickly.

You can hear the difference by counting 1,2,3,4,1,2,3,4 and then counting 1,2,3,1,2,3.

Whether you speed up the tempo, or slow it down, the difference in the feel of the two time signatures is still the same.

In bars 7 and 8 there are two dotted half notes; meaning that the half note gets a 1, 2, count (as it always does) and the dot is worth half of whatever note it follows, in this case, the half note.

Since the half note is worth two counts and the dot is worth one count, this completes a bar in 3/4 time.

The note is played on the 1 count and held until the 3 count is completed.

If a dot (.) follows a dot (..); the second dot equals 1/2 the note value of the first dot.

Practice this passage (bars 9 through 12) as often as you can.

Begin by playing at a very slow tempo and gradually begin to increase your speed.

After you have mastered this passage, it will give you a good understanding of playing in 3/4 time.

In 3/4 time, you will not often find sixteenth notes (although there will be times) because they are very difficult to play in this time signature.

Once again, if you find sixteenth notes written in 3/4 time, they will probably be written for strings, drums, or horns although they're sometimes written as piano parts.

In bars 5, 6, 12, and 14, notice that there are some accidentals, in the form of (♯'s).

These sharps (♯'s) are on the F, C, and D notes; meaning that they signify a particular key or scale.

Referring back to the section on key signatures, you will find that there is no key signature containing sharps on the notes F, C, and D, in *that* order, but there is a key signature that contains the order of F♯, C♯, G♯, D♯.

That is the key of E major, but could this be E major when there is no G♯?

This is *definitely* the key of E major, as we shall prove it.

These are some of the reasons you can be positive that this music is in the key of E major.

If you try to find a flat key (a key containing flats) using G♭, D♭ and E♭, (which are the opposite of F♯, C♯, and D♯) there is no such key.

In a flat key signature, you must have a B♭, because that is the first flat in the order of flats.

If there is no B♭, then the music is most likely not in a flat key.

However if there is an F♯, and no B♭, the music is in a sharp key, because F♯ is the first sharp in the order of sharps and B♭ is the first flat in the order of flats.

Key Signature of E major

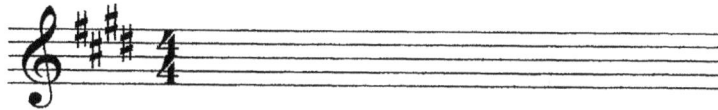

Although, the key signature for the key (or scale) of E major is F♯, C♯, G♯, and D♯, and the passage only has the F♯, C♯, and D♯, it just means that the melody didn't contain a G♯, and, since all of the other elements are in place, the music is in the key of E major.

If the music were to continue, and there happens to be a G note in the melody, then it will be G♯.

What you have just learned, is how to find the key that a melody is in, by checking for the number of sharps or flats.

Whatever the *correct* order of sharps or flats turn out to be, will give you the key of the music, allowing you to know which chords to select from.

If you've ever wondered how someone can sing a few notes, and then have a total stranger accompany them on an instrument, this is the method that they use.

The few notes of the melody allow the accompanist to find the key, thereby, finding the chords.

121

To sum things up, try these chords, taken from the E major scale, over the melody.

This is, once again, proof that this melody is indeed in the key of E major.

To find the key, by examining the melody, will require a knowledge of the order of (♯'s & ♭'s) in the key signatures.

This may be a bit difficult, at first, but keep on trying until you can remember what order they come in.

If you write a melody and the sharps or flats do not line up with a key signature, there are a few things that you can try.

Find out if, perhaps, you have most of the sharps or flats in a particular key signature.

EXAMPLE :

F, G♯ , A♯ ,C , D♯

In this example sharps were used because the melody is ascending (moving up).

If you will observe closely, the melody begins with an F note, giving you your first indication that the melody is not in a sharp key.

Why?

Because a sharp key would have an F♯ as it's first ♯ in the key signature, and here you already have an F natural.

The next thing to do would be to try the sharp notes as flat notes. (A♭, B♭, E♭)

From this we can see that, although not in proper order, these are the flats in the key signature of E♭.

If everything else lines up and one or two notes do not, it might be better to change the one or two notes to make them fit into a key.

Once you become familiar with how music *should* sound, it becomes easier to hear wrong notes right away.

When you feel that you have found the proper key, for your melody, try some of the chords, from that key, along with the melody.

In music, there are quite a few symbols, used to help us to achieve certain musical expressions.

Let's examine some of them, starting with the tie.

EXAMPLE 1

The slightly curved lines used to join some of the notes in the above example are called ties.

As their name implies, they are used to tie two or more, (usually two) notes together.

By tying the notes together, you are actually helping to sustain the first note.

When a tie is used to join two notes that are the same, melodically, the first note is held down until the value of both notes is completed.

In bar 2 a whole note could actually have done the job better.

EXAMPLE 1:

In example 1, above, there are two unfamilar signs.

The first one is the triplet sign, indicated by the number 3 above, or below a group of three notes.

What this means is that these three notes, together, occupies one beat of whatever time signature they happen to come under, in this case, a quarter note.

From looking at these notes they appear to be three eighth notes, and they are, but the interpretation of them is different from three normal eighth notes.

Here's the reason why; the 3 written over the stems of the notes call for a type of rhythmic feel.

Where three eighth notes in a 4/4 time signature would normally be played as 1 & 2, these three eighth notes cannot be played that way, because the two beat is occupied by a quarter note.

Obviously the playing of *all* of *these* notes will have to be completed on the one beat.

The only way to get this done is by playing them with the feel of a bar of 3/4.

In other words, count off 1,2,3,4 as a lead-in, and on the 1 of the actual first bar of the example, count a quick 1,2,3 on the one beat, count the two beat as a normal two beat, count a quick 1,2,3, on the three beat, and count the four beat as a normal four beat.

Triplets occupy the same space that *two* notes of that value would normally occupy.

In the example above, the triplets *(3 eighth notes)* occupy the same space that *two eighth notes* would normally occupy.

EXAMPLE 1:

Going back to this example; another sign that you might be unfamiliar with, is the repeat sign, at the end of bar 2.

It is used to indicate just what it's name implies, a repeat of whatever came before it.

A repeat sign at the end of a bar means for the reader to go back to the beginning of the music and play until the point of the repeat sign.

Play these examples, as often as possible, to help you to develop your agility, reading, and to help you to understand composing.

Once you begin to learn how the music is brought together and the principles governing music, you will be able to express your own musical ideas.

These examples will be explored further on the following pages.

EXAMPLE 1

EXAMPLE 2

EXAMPLE 3

EXAMPLE 4

EXAMPLE 1

From observing this example, we can see that there are no ♯'s or ♭'s, indicating that the piece is more than likely in the key of C major.

Investigating further, we can see that there is no F note and no B note, being the first notes in the sharp and flat keys, respectively.

Moving to the next note in the sharp key signatures (C♯), we find that there are 4 C notes present in the piece, but none of them are sharp.

Having no F♯, and C notes that are not sharp, rules out a sharp key signature.

Also containing no B♭ and 3 E notes that are not flat, rules out a flat key signature.

Since the music seems to be in the key of C major, let's try using a C chord beneath the melody.

By playing the G note of the C chord on the bottom, we can keep the C chord in close proximity to the melody.

See the example on the next page.

128

R. H.

L. H.

By playing the C chord in 2nd inversion form (G note on the bottom), we can keep the chord notes and the melody notes from overlapping until the fourth beat of the third bar.

That is the reason for not sustaining the chord for the complete third bar, if we do, the E note in the chord would be the exact same note as the E note in the melody.

One of the notes would have to be left out and the note that's likely to be missed the most is the melody note.

Notice that, in the third bar, the fingering changes.

In order to accommodate the E note in the melody, *with the right hand;* while the 2 finger is playing the A note, quickly slide the 1 finger in position to come down on the E note.

Since the 1 finger can't get back to the G note quickly enough to make a smoothe transition, the 2 finger is now used to play the G note.

Even though this example has the the appearance of being in the key of D major, because of the F♯ and the C♯, it really is not.

To be sure, for yourself, try some of the tonic functioning chords from the key of D major.

Now, since A major is the next scale in the order of sharp key signatures (F♯, C♯, and G♯), let's try an A chord with this melody.

R. H.

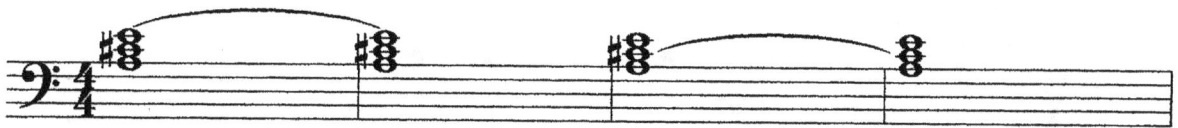

L. H.

Once you've tried the A major chord along with this melody, it is obvious that this piece of music is in the key of A major, without a G♯ in the melody.

Try to keep chord positions separate from melodies, so as not to take away from either of them.

It would be a shame to have a nice melody interrupted because a chord needs one of your melody notes, and vice versa.

There are enough notes to go around, so use good taste.

This melody has been transposed down, by an octave, so that the chord could be played in the upper register of the keyboard and not interfere with the melody notes.

The reason that we chose to use a C M7 over this melody is to accommodate the frequent occurance of the B note.

The C M7 gives the B note more of a reason to be there, so to speak.

For playing the melody, you have the option of two different fingerings.

You can alternate between them, for the sake of practice.

These are different ways to play EXAMPLE 4 ; one with the chords on top, and one with the melody on top.

In the second example above, notice that a quarter rest comes on the 1 beat of bars 1 and 3.

The reason for leaving out the first note is that the F note in the chord takes the place of the F note in the melody, since they are in the same register (area) of the keyboard.

To show what a difference inversions can make, let's try some experiments.

First of all, let's take a C chord and play it in the root position, 1rst inversion position, the 2nd inversion position, then back to the root position.

Going back to a chord progression that we played previously, let's try playing each of the chords in the 1rst inversion.

Next, let's alternate by playing the chords in root position, 2nd inversion, root position, 2nd inversion, root position, and 2nd inversion.

I hope you have begun to see the many possibilities that are available to you, through the use of different inversions.

You would probably expect all of the notes in a chord to always have the same time duration, but they don't always have to.

EXAMPLE:
In The Key Of C Major

This example contains C major chords built upon every beat of the bar.

Even though the half - note (G) in the bass clef is only played on the 1 count, it is sustained (held down) until the 2 count is completed.

So, in essence, while it appears that only the quarter - notes (C & E) in the treble clef are played on the 2 count, the (G) in the bass clef completes the C major chord, because it is still sounding on the 2 count.

The same principle applies when the half - note (E) is played on the 3 count in the treble clef.

It is sustained until the 4 count is finished and combines with the (G & C) in the bass clef to complete a C major chord.

You can see how this could apply to other combinations of notes as well.

Note that sometimes the stems of the notes and chords are pointing up and at other times they are pointing down.

The reason for this is to avoid clutter and to keep the music *looking* good, *it has nothing to do with sound.*

Also be aware that in Bar 2, all of the notes on each beat are part of a C major chord built on that particular beat.

The C chord built upon the first beat of Bar 2 is different from the rest of the chords in that it contains two of the same note (E), one in the treble clef and one in the bass clef, it is also a four note chord.

EXAMPLE:
<u>In The Key Of C Major</u>

Learn to try different voicings for chords to see which ones suit *your* preference, thereby creating your own style and sound.

Bar 2 shows a few ways to play a C major chord, but you might like the way some of them sound and others you might not care for; this is why you are encouraged to experiment.

Remember that, although some notes might not be joined together on the same stem or written in the same clef, if they fall on the same beat, they are to be played at the same time, making them a chord.

136

1rst Inversions & Root Positions In C Major

R= root   position
1 = first   inversion
2 = second   inversion

A friend of mine once said to me, "It's great to be able to read music, but even better to be able to write it."

These studies are meant to prepare you to have the ability to do both.

Now that we are at the end of the book, I can say, without fear of scaring some of you, that music is very similar to mathematics.

If you haven't already figured it out, the best way to remember certain things, is to think in terms of patterns, which are very much a part of music.

These studies are designed to make this learning experience as easy, informative, and as enjoyable as possible, while at the same time empowering the student with musical expression.

I have tried to think of any question that one could possibly ask and to answer them all.

Once you've completed this book, there are lot's of other books that will supplement and enhance your musical endeavors.

Thank you for studying with us and we hope that we have helped to enable you, musically.

Sincerely,

Jay McGee